Home Front Baltimore

To John, with best wishes
from the author,

Gilbert Sandler

HOME FRONT BALTIMORE

An Album of Stories from World War II

Gilbert Sandler

THE JOHNS HOPKINS UNIVERSITY PRESS   BALTIMORE

© 2011 The Johns Hopkins University Press
All rights reserved. Published 2011
Printed in the United States of America on
acid-free paper
9 8 7 6 5 4 3 2 1

The Johns Hopkins University Press
2715 North Charles Street
Baltimore, Maryland 21218-4363
www.press.jhu.edu

Library of Congress Cataloging-in-
Publication Data

Sandler, Gilbert.
    Home front Baltimore : an album of
stories from World War II / Gilbert Sandler.
        p. cm.
    Includes bibliographical references and
index.
    ISBN-13: 978-0-8018-9983-6 (hardcover :
alk. paper)
    ISBN-10: 0-8018-9983-4 (hardcover : alk.
paper)
    1. World War, 1939–1945—Maryland—
Baltimore. 2. World War, 1939–1945—Social
aspects—Maryland—Baltimore. 3. Baltimore (Md.)—History—20th century.
4. Baltimore (Md.)—Social conditions—20th
century. 5. World War, 1939–1945—Personal narratives, American.   I. Title.
    D769.85.M31B367 2011
    940.53'7526—dc22   2010046808

A catalog record for this book is available
from the British Library.

Illustrations on pages 88, 93 (image
#Z24-1733), 96 (top), 117, 119–21, and 133
are reprinted courtesy of the Maryland
Historical Society; on pages 43, 49, 84 (bottom), 103, and 124 (bottom), courtesy of
the Baltimore Streetcar Museum; on page
90, courtesy of the Library of Congress. All
other illustrations are reprinted courtesy of
the Baltimore Sun Media Group.

*Special discounts are available for bulk
purchases of this book. For more information,
please contact Special Sales at 410-516-6936
or specialsales@press.jhu.edu.*

The Johns Hopkins University Press uses
environmentally friendly book materials,
including recycled text paper that is composed of at least 30 percent post-consumer
waste, whenever possible. All of our book
papers are acid-free, and our jackets and
covers are printed on paper with recycled
content.

To Joan

Contents

Preface

On a spring day in 2006 I found myself in the library of the *Baltimore Sun,* doing research for my weekly editorial page column, "Baltimore Glimpses." As I rifled through back editions, the issue of June 20, 1944, caught my attention. It was "D + 5" of the battle of Saipan, known as Operation Forager, designed to take control of the Mariana Islands, and I was serving aboard the USS *Leonis,* AK-128 (Attack Cargo Class), engaged in that operation. As part of Task Force 34.1, under the command of Adm. Raymond Spruance, we helped land as many as twenty thousand troops in less than three weeks. Before the operation was completed, more than three thousand Americans had died. Reading through the *Baltimore Sun*—mornings, evenings, Sundays—it struck me that during those same weeks the Orioles were moving into and out of first place in the International League, that it was a heady time in the town. I could picture the standing-room-only crowds, and the cheering, and the fans munching peanuts and popcorn and sipping soft drinks. (No beer allowed on municipal property!) I thought about the contrasts—over here, over there.

The searches became habit forming, the question more tantalizing: what was going on during those war years in my hometown while I was away from it? I continued to wander further into this world of juxtapositions, exploring the comparables for differences in place and tone. In August 1942, when bandleader Tommy Dorsey was performing on the stage of the Hippodrome Theater on Eutaw Street, American prisoners of war were, at pretty much the same time, performing *Julius Caesar* on a jury-rigged stage in Burma. On February 23, 1945, when marines raised the Stars and Stripes atop Mount Suribachi on Iwo Jima for Joe Rosenthal's famous picture, representatives of the National Association for the Advancement of Colored People in Baltimore raised an issue before the Baltimore City School Board: they insisted that to assure better quality of education for Baltimore's African American students, the "Negro schools must be operated by Negroes." So it went.

The deeper I got into the project, the more I realized: *Reading* about the home front was not going to do it for me—satisfy my curiosity about what was going on in Baltimore's home front while I was not there to experience it. Reading it, I wasn't *getting* it. I needed to *talk* to people. I sensed that all the words ever written about such wrenching times, all the pictures presenting them, could not take the place of one person's encounter with them.

But who in the world was still around to talk to? People who had lived through those years (1941-45), at least as young adults, had to have been born in the 1920s, putting them currently in their mid to late eighties, some into their nineties. And to narrow the circle of possibilities, I wanted all points of view—from rich and poor, old and young, white and black, and they had not only to be willing to talk about home front Baltimore but also to have retained memories of it and be able to find words to convey feelings, share confidences, and make me a traveler with them on this journey back into a very special time of their lives. Finding people to talk to was a challenge, but it was the only way I knew to augment the literature and to bring it alive, capture the mood of the era, get it all down on paper, and write this book.

I got lucky. I found myself, due to changing life circumstances, living in Roland Park Place, a retirement community situated between Roland Park and Hampden (where I spent a few nights at the bar of the local VFW). It was among the populations of both communities that I discovered people who told me what I needed to know. In every case we talked for hours, and although many if not most of the interviews did not work out, those that did enabled me to get to know the powerful emotional responses that were insufficiently conveyed by the written word. I had to hear them recalled wistfully, exclaimed joyfully, or even cried through. As I read of an event, or an episode, or a civic mood that defined the home front, I would ask people how, in each case, they remembered it—on a very personal level. When they came through for me it was often with undisguised passion. Mrs. Louisa

Reynolds, remembering air raid warnings: "Those screaming sirens …Who-o-o-o-e-e-e…And the relief I felt when the siren rang out an all clear." You have to have heard Mrs. Reynolds as I did, her voice trembling, to understand the fear, the relief, she was talking about. And, in contrast, to hear Mrs. Katherine "Kat" Fletcher recalling: "My family never seemed to suffer from shortages. I don't remember the war as a time of loss or sacrifice. I'm not defending that. It's just the way it was." I was getting the divergent views I was looking for—from the patriots to the black-marketers; from those who worried constantly and from those who thought life on the home front a lighthearted exercise in inconvenience. (Later on I explain why home front Baltimore reminded me of the Christmas windows of Hochschild Kohn's and Hutzler's department stores in the 1940s.)

So, working over some two years, I was better able to understand the stories I had been reading about simply by talking with people who had lived them. From many small stories coming together in this way came one big story, *Home Front Baltimore: An Album of Stories from World War II.*

A word about dates and times: This book is not a history. It is drawn, largely, from newspaper reports and personal memories. It is a collection of stories, and its structure is the choice of the collector alone. The techniques are more the journalist's than the historian's— so the book contains as many memories as citations. I choose to tell these stories about *Home Front Baltimore* by setting out the contrasts between what was happening over here in Baltimore and what was happening "over there." The dates I use are Eastern Standard or Eastern War Time, but battles, victories, and defeats happened in other time zones—"forward" (eastward) in the case of Europe, "back" (westward) in the case of the Pacific, and yet a whole different day beyond the International Date Line. I discovered early on that continually adjusting for differing time zones and still holding to the story line would get me bogged down in the details of longitude and in the dizzying concept of the date line. So, in drawing these contrasts, I have taken liberties: when I say a certain thing happened "at the same time," the reader will understand that I mean *more or less* at the same time. I can only hope purists will understand the difference between history and a storyteller's version of it. For that understanding, I am grateful.

Always, men at war are confronted with the simultaneity of life in both a world at war *and* a world distanced from war, and, when made aware of it, find the incongruities striking. Sgt. William Quinn, going home for R&R after eight months serving in Iraq, wrote in the *Washington Post* (November 11, 2007) that he found himself in the Detroit airport heading for the baggage claim, and he observed: "I watched travelers walking, and talking on their cell phones, chatting with friends and acting just the way people had before I'd left for Baghdad. The war just didn't seem to be taking place in another country; it seemed to be taking place in another universe. There I was in desert camouflage, wondering how all the intensity, how the violence, how the tears and the killing in Iraq, could really be happening at the same time that all of these people were hurrying to catch their flights to Los Angeles or wherever." How indeed?

Sergeant Quinn had picked up on the unsettling and haunting phenomenon that I was wrestling with: The striking contrasts between what was happening over there, and, at the same time, over here (in Baltimore), during World War II. I draw no moral or meaning from the juxtapositions. The reader is on his or her own.

People at home during a war can never really know war; they must be forever at a remove from it. But men at war, far from home, remember only too well what life was like at home when they left it, and so the contrasts, when they read of them in these pages, are going to weigh heavily.

This is history by contrasts—over here with over there, and within and among the home fronts in Baltimore during World War II. I like to think that this technique of telling the story provides a deeper understanding of it and a closer-to-home-and-hearth history of a very special, transformative, and long-ago time and place.

Home Front Baltimore

Baltimore was at war before America was. At the Glenn L. Martin Company in Middle River, employees turned out the aircraft that figured heavily in the fight against the Axis powers well before the United States entered the war. Martin himself later made a speech in which he boasted that his company was "the largest aircraft manufacturer in the United States, if not the world."

★ ★ ★ PREPAREDNESS

At first, there were three wars for Baltimoreans to think about. One was the shooting war—distant, in a Europe far away (in the era before jet planes); then there was the "war" close at hand—soldiers and sailors crowding the streets and streetcars and restaurants and taverns and movies and everywhere and inescapably the burgeoning work force that had come to town to produce Martin bombers and Liberty ships and parts for every kind of instrument and machine designed for war. This struggle to make war changed the physical and cultural landscape of the city. But there was yet a third war: The isolationists made it, arguing "Keep America Out of War!"

What did you do before you were a soldier?

Early in 1941 the Baltimore City Department of Recreation, whose members apparently knew raging hormones when they saw them, embarked on a plan to organize dances for the throngs of young soldiers and sailors who—lonely, knowing no one, far from home—walked the streets of Baltimore "looking for something to do."

So on the night of January 25, 1941, the department sent eighty young women, whom the *Sun* described as "carefully selected and recommended by the Young Men's and Young Women's Christian Association, the Young Men's and Young Women's Hebrew Association, and a federation of churches and allied organizations," on a bus ride to Edgewood Arsenal. There, in collaboration with army authorities, the young ladies attended one of the very first staged socials for visiting servicemen and women in the Baltimore region. Officials got it right:

Changing shifts at Glenn L. Martin early in 1941, when more than fifty-three thousand men and women worked at Martin in three shifts, around the clock, seven days a week. Drawn in huge numbers from the entire mid-Atlantic region, they created a crushing housing shortage. The company itself helped to solve the problem: It worked in collaboration with contractors to build residential communities called Mars Estates, Victory Villa Gardens, Kingsley Park, Stansbury Manor, Aero Acres, and Riverdale. The streets had names like Propeller Drive, Kitty Hawk Road, Rip Cord Street, and Fuselage Lane. Martin's not only built bombers, it built bomber-makers' homes.

to keep Edgewood soldiers from looking for girls in Baltimore, send the girls from Baltimore to Edgewood.

Mrs. Ruth G. Ehlers, departmental supervisor for social relations, took charge of obtaining dancing companions and entertainment for the soldiers. Hers was the job of building up a file of names of young women who would receive invitations.

Mrs. Ehlers's ambition was to send a busload of the young ladies to a nearby army base almost every night of the week. She made clear that the invitation list was generated with great care and that a dozen or so organizations had been asked to recommend "personable young women."

"Each bus," she said, "will have a chaperone, who will check off the names as the girls enter. There will be no gate crashing. Each group of young ladies who make up a full bus will be representing a cross section of city life. There will be a certain percentage of Protestant girls, some Catholic, some Jewish."

Mary Hortop was one of those young ladies. "Ruth Garber Ehlers

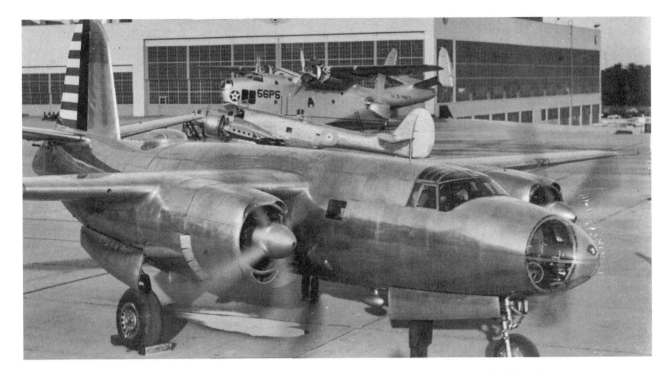

The pride of the Martin fleet parked in front of a hangar in Middle River, January 1941. *Back to front,* a patrol bomber (PBM) for the U.S. Navy, an attack bomber for the British, and a B-26 medium bomber, destined for the U.S. Army Air Force.

was a good friend of my mother," she recalled, "and so I went on some of Mrs. Ehlers's trips and on some of those led by my mother. The soldiers we met were a mixed bag—the young fellows wanted companions for vigorous dancing, and the older fellows just wanted company for a while. I was always better at talking than at dancing, so I was often paired up with older men and those who were awkward on the dance floor and really wanted someone to talk with. I learned some tricks to start conversations: 'What did you do before you were in the army?' If they said, 'Guess!' I would ask to look at their hands. The ones who had done physical labor were evident, like the man whose fingers were permanently stained black in the creases. He had been a stove blacker who went from house to house in the country, blacking the big iron stoves favored by the farm wives. He enjoyed finding someone to talk to who found that interesting. I thought he was intelligent and different. And I still remember when a fellow of forty or so answered my, 'What did you do before you were a soldier?' question with a grin. He said, 'I was a Kotex salesman.' I grinned back and said, 'On behalf of the women of America, I thank you.' And we danced happily on.

"Often the soldiers would have photos of their wives or sweethearts. Some were cute young girls and others were middle-aged

The 175th Infantry saddles up on the morning of February 18, 1941. Composed mostly of recruits with little more military experience than two weeks in Baltimore's Fifth Regiment Armory, the unit arrived at Fort George Gordon Meade that same afternoon. The *Sun* reported that "smoke poured from the chimney of brand-new company kitchens here this afternoon in a message to the Twenty-ninth Division's entire cantonment that the 175th infantry had moved in from Baltimore."

Cooks went to work immediately. By suppertime, every man was served a hot meal. The menu: beef stew, split pea soup with croutons, sliced pickles, corn fritters, vegetable salad, gingerbread, bread and butter, and coffee. Not bad for army food.

women. If they were pretty, my response was easy. If they looked like tired, plain women, it was harder. But just to have a chance to talk about this woman back home seemed to make a fellow feel good."

Mrs. Ehlers did not mention cataloging the girls as blonds or brunettes and said she "doubted it would come to that. The only thing the boys ask is that the girls be young, cute, and know how to dance."

The dances were scheduled to begin at 8:30 in the evening and end at 11:30. Then the girls were to board the bus for home and their civilian lives, the soldiers to return to their barracks and the army routine.

"The evening's activities," Mrs. Ehlers insisted, "remained under strict supervision." But Mrs. Ehlers had never been a young soldier, alone in an unfamiliar city, far from home.

In the spring of 1941, especially on Saturday afternoons and nights, downtown was shoulder to shoulder with soldiers and sailors. They came in from Aberdeen Proving Ground, Edgewood Arsenal, Fort Holabird, Fort Meade, the Bainbridge Naval Training Station in Cecil County, and probably elsewhere.

The *Sun* decided to invite two men from Company G, Seventieth Tank Battalion, up from Fort Meade and send them about the city's landmark points of interest in the company of the paper's masterful

Saturday Leave . . . Meade Soldiers In Baltimore

Baltimore's "sights" and places of entertainment are becoming more and more the mecca of the military as Maryland's camps steadily swell with the draftees who are being called into service in increasing numbers. From the army posts in the north, Aberdeen and Edgewood, from nearby Holabird and from Fort George G. Meade, the new soldiers reach the city each week-end, pleasure bound—at least as far as their limited resources will permit. Here is the saga of one such week-end, enjoyed by two privates who are now receiving their compulsory military training.

THE ARRIVAL
Privates James Cochran and Edward Kundrot, of Company G, Seventieth Tank Battalion, reach Camden Station from Fort Meade.

FUELING UP
Before starting "the big push" through Baltimore, they do a little eating. Cochran, 19, is from Columbus. Kundrot's from Wilkes-Barre

SIGHT-SEEING
Somehow the boys couldn't stay away from—here they are at Fort McHenry with Cap— whose father is an army chaplain with the of Captain, taking Kundrot's picture

HISTORICAL RESEARCH
On Charles street, the two privates visit the Washington Monument, get a view from the top, see the exhibits in the rooms at the base

A LITTLE CULTURE
Edward, who worked for a Wilkes-Barre bottling plant and drove a department store truck, and James, who worked in a men's clothing store, pause at the Museum of Art

EXPERIMENTAL EATING
Now the Ohioan is trying his first raw oyster aboard a Pratt street boat while a little later (right) Edward tried out some Italian food—with indifferent success. The problem of eating seems to have been a major concern of the day

CAME THE NIGHT
As the sun set the lights flashed on over the Lexington street theaters and lured the soldiers twain into seeing the latest Hollywood had to offer

FUN AT THE "Y"
Privates Kundrot and Cochran find themselves at the Y. M. C. A. dance for visiting soldiers. Their partner of the moment is Miss Mildred Wishard

REFRESHMENTS
Now the two soldiers, neither of whom smokes nor drinks, have taken their dates soda fountain for refreshment. The second "date" is Miss Nancy Kain

PENNY ARCADE
Cochran, who volunteered for military service, tries a game of skill while Kundrot, who was drawn in the draft lottery, at the age of 22, looks on

IN "THE BLOCK"
Where the lights burn the brightest—and longest—the boys, forgetting the big guns at Fort McHenry, have found a way to test their marksmanship

END OF A PERFECT DAY
Back at Camden Station, James and Edward keep a late date with Morpheus waiting for the 1.15 to leave for the fort

Greek women in national costume sell tickets in front of the Hippodrome Theater, Monday evening, March 31, 1941, to benefit Greek War Relief. *Front row, left to right:* Mrs. Andrew T. Cavacos, Katherine N. Konstant, Helen Poule, and Mrs. Peter T. Capsanes. *Back row, left to right:* Mrs. Mario Psaros, Mary Perentesis, Mary Apostol, Irene Barkega, and Helen Lengares.

Nicholas Prevas, a historian of Baltimore's Greek community, explained the background to the ladies' ticket selling: "The heroic resistance of the Greek people to the Italian invasion had aroused the admiration of the world. The world could now see that though some European countries had succumbed to the Axis powers, Greeks had subdued the invading Italian army, and around the world the Greeks found a new sense of confidence and staged fund-raising rallies in support of Greece. It turned out that Baltimore's Greek community was among the most active of those communities in the national Greek War Relief effort."

Parishioners had received an initial solicitation letter from the parish's Fr. Joaquin Papachristous and Parish Council president George Karengela. "The horrible and bloody drama of Europeans now being staged in our beautiful Hellas, the Land of Light, the root of civilization, the Mother of Democracy, Immortal Greece suffers the oppression of greedy and hateful dictators of Europe," read the missive. "The strong government of Greece with her heroic children answers in typical Grecian manner: 'We will not give in!'"

Changing times called for changing roles for women, like changing flat tires on passenger cars on the home front while the guys were changing tires on Jeeps at the war fronts. Here, on May 9, 1941, demonstrating what a young lady in war must learn to do, Mrs. Irene Grzech, of the Red Cross Motor Corps, makes it all seem easy.

photographer, Aubrey Bodine. We do not know if Pvts. James Cochrun, of Columbus, Ohio, and Edward Kundrot, of Wilkes-Barre, Pennsylvania, both nineteen years old, actually *volunteered* for this assignment, but in newspaper coverage they seemed agreeable to it.

They arrived at Camden Station late on the morning of March 29, and the first thing they did, exercising gustatory freedom, was to sit down at the refreshment counter in the station and order some civilian-cooked food—in this case, hot dogs and hamburgers. A well-meaning civilian taking in the scene (or the *Sun*'s features editor) suggested that they first visit Fort McHenry, and though it seemed like a busman's holiday, they did—taking pictures of themselves sitting on cannon, as if they were ordinary tourists.

All relief agencies became expert at raising money for, and community interest in, a war that America had until then escaped. Supporting the British during the air battle for their "island fortress," Bundles for Britain put this captured Messerschmitt—pride of the Luftwaffe, bane of the Royal Air Force—on display at the Maryland Theater, which in 1941 was on Howard just above Franklin. The downtown moviegoing and shopping crowd could not easily miss the exhibit. The Maryland stood next door to the Stanley Theater, which the same day the *Sun* published this photograph, July 11, 1941, played *The Bride Came C.O.D,* starring Dorothy Lamour and Jon Hall.

Next stop was Mount Vernon Place and the Washington Monument. The soldiers climbed to the top of the shaft, took in that splendid view of the city, spread out below in all directions, and then spent some time in the first-floor lobby, taking in the exhibits. From there, it was a few minutes drive up North Charles Street to the Baltimore Museum of Art. In civilian life Kundrot had worked for a bottling plant and driven a department store truck; Cochrun had worked in a men's clothing store. Of course, they may have been ardent art lovers. Or maybe they were only beginning their training in art history. In any case, this day on Art Museum Drive they answered the call to cultural duty and seriously contemplated the works of Matisse and van Gogh.

Chow time in Baltimore called for a Baltimore-style lunch, which in the case of the two visiting privates meant, first, oysters at a Pratt Street restaurant, followed by a huge tomato-and-meat-sauce spaghetti dinner in Little Italy.

After dinner, a walk into downtown was a must, to see the flashing neon lights and watch wartime Baltimore at play. After a movie on Lexington Street, the soldiers asked what soldiers on leave can be counted on to ask: Where are the girls and where are the dances? They found both at the YMCA at Franklin and Cathedral streets, and the published account even provided the names of the dancing partners they met there—Miss Nancy Kaiss and Miss Mildred Wishard. That was in 1941; where are they now?

Inevitably, Kundrot and Cochrun went down to Baltimore's famous and some would say infamous Block—that winking, blinking stretch of movie houses, shooting galleries, tattoo parlors, and exotic night clubs along East Baltimore Street from Guilford Avenue to the Fallsway. The record shows only that they tried their skills in the shooting galleries and their luck in the penny arcades.

By midnight the young privates were half asleep on hard benches in Camden Station, waiting for the 1:15 a.m. bus back to Fort Meade, carrying with them a few stories to tell barracks mates. We do not know which stories they told.

You learn to enjoy working more than you do going to coming-out parties

"Say farewell to the old type of debutante," a young one told a *Sun* reporter on July 9, 1941, "and good riddance for all concerned. She really didn't have half so much fun as her working sister of today." Another debutante said, "You have no time for dances, for all-night parties, and the like when you have to be at a war plant at eight in the morning. You learn to enjoy *working* more than you do going to coming-out parties."

Mrs. Charles O'Donovan, director of the placement service of the Junior League (a group of young ladies from society committed to volunteer for community causes), endorsed the view. She said that more than 90 percent of the younger members of the league were working or studying for jobs. "Most young women feel that the future is very uncertain. They want to prepare themselves as well as possible to meet changing conditions. Many of them also are working for patriotic reasons. They honestly want to play their own small parts in the nation's total effort.

"Of course, there are many who are not working for pay. They have given up the usual round of parties for the hard work of being a full-time nurse's aide or a laboratory technician. They are active in

A familiar sight outside Baltimore in 1941: soldiers, many of them national guardsmen, doing what they were convinced they were doing too much of—marching. Here an antitank company of the 175th Infantry, on the morning of July 31, 1941, moves along on a seventy-five-mile march on the Lewistown-Frederick Road, west and north of Baltimore. At the end of the day, cold water felt heavenly on aching feet.

On August 2, 1941, a parade organized
by the Committee to Defend America (and put isolationists to shame)
coursed through the city streets and
made the newspaper. Maria Dabney,
of Lancaster, Pennsylvania, proudly
played the part of Miss Liberty.

For many war workers, employment at the sprawling Glenn L. Martin plant in eastern Baltimore County meant living close by with their families in a trailer home in a trailer park. Often, husband and wife worked separate shifts. Here, husband and father Jack Finell holds his nineteen-month-old son, Reid, while his wife holds six-month-old Glenn. "The first two hundred families moved in to what was being called the very first U.S. trailer camp, out on Eastern Avenue, on the afternoon of August 7, 1941," the *Sun* reported. "One housewife said, 'It won't be a soft life, no bed of roses, but it will provide clean, comfortable quarters nearer to jobs than anything most of

the workers have found so far, and far cleaner.'"

The trailer park consisted of one hundred trailers for families of four, and about a hundred smaller ones for couples. Each rented for $6.50 per week, which included water and electricity. Single men lived in dormitories nearby.

"People got into line as early as dawn to sign leases, get their keys, and prepare to move in. The office stayed open until near midnight taking care of latecomers," testified the *Sun*. "Families continued moving in until late last night." Moving in proved to be less difficult than many anticipated; much of the needed furniture and

many fixtures had been built in to the trailers, so it was mostly a matter of handling clothes, personal effects, cooking utensils, and tableware.

At the end of the day, Mrs. David Dolbin of Harrisburg, Pennsylvania, resting with her children—Joan, eight, and David, nine—told a reporter, "I think we'll all just go into town and have some supper." For the Dolbin family and 199 families like them, it had been a very long, hard day. Whatever one had been used to, wherever in America these tenants had come from, this trailer park out Eastern Avenue in Baltimore County was what they now called home—for the duration.

There's no place like home, even if home is a trailer park. Families thrust together in these tight living spaces soon organized their own community council, which decided to permit cats and dogs. Planners spaced water mains evenly throughout the park, each with a length of hose to reach each trailer, or most of them. Community toilets, bathing/laundry facilities, and telephones were available. Ice trucks made their rounds with ice. Milkmen served each trailer, door to door. Oil- or kerosene-burning stoves provided heat.

civilian defense and in the Red Cross. The energy they once put into the social world now goes into serious, useful work."

All we had to do was step off base and stick out a thumb!

In 1941, James "Jim" Bready was a twenty-two-year-old private first class whom the army had sent from Minnesota to Edgewood Arsenal, a Chemical Warfare Service installation about twenty miles northeast of Baltimore. "When we were off duty, on a good-weather evening or a weekend," he recalled, "we headed for the big city—with its cinemas and burlesque shows, its restaurants, stores, amusement parks, and USOs.

"But how we got to Baltimore, and back to the barracks afterward, was a phenomenon of the war—one that changed lives. Few enlisted men had automobiles of their own, and public transportation seldom served military bases. So we hitchhiked. We'd stand there, outside the post perimeter, alongside Route 40, patiently waiting—and confident that a passing car or truck would put on its brakes and offer one or more of us a lift. All we had to do was step off base and stick out a thumb! It was the uniform that did it—olive drab in winter, khaki in summer.

"All over Baltimore, beside the main highways, you would see

First Separate Company of African American soldiers in the Maryland National Guard in training at Fort Dix, New Jersey, in July of 1941. African Americans had served in this company as far back as 1882. The army eventually ordered the company to active status, putting it on guard duty in the United States until, late in the war, it went to the Pacific. The war ended before it saw combat.

A Sunpapers photographer captured this pleasant moment in the Separate Company barracks as the men had some fun after a grueling training day. Clearly, in some cases, the unit that marches together can make music together.

soldiers and sailors, marines and airmen, hoping for a free ride and, generally, not having to wait long. For civilian drivers, it was a great way to express gratitude to guys who might soon be going overseas, to the front lines.

"Yes, there was a degree of risk. The armed forces had that early a.m. ceremony called reveille and roll call. Failure to be present made you subject to punishment. But Baltimore was worth it all.

"While stationed at Edgewood, I made it one day to Richmond and back. Another time, to Boston and back. Later on, while stationed in Washington and on a week's furlough, I once hitched to Iowa and back.

"Something else about it cheered us. Hitchhiking was the prerogative of enlisted personnel. For the brass, it would be demeaning— a commissioned officer standing out on Route 40, begging with his thumb? Nah. So while an enlisted man could get around off the base fairly easily, an officer might have to labor through cumbersome procedures to arrange for transportation. That contrast made us GIs feel good.

"You're in the army now"—for sure!
Draftees from the mid-Atlantic region
now in the 175th Infantry arrived at
A. P. Hill military reservation in Virginia,
September 18, 1941.

"While exploring Baltimore, I stopped in one day at the Govans Branch of the Enoch Pratt Free Library. And started talking books and authors with the pert, red-haired young lady behind the desk. She said her name was Mary Hortop, and she would soon begin her senior year at Eastern High School. I walked her home—her father, I was to learn, had been stationed at Edgewood in World War I. Amazing, how high I was beginning to rate Baltimore—and how often I was soon hitch-hiking between Edgewood Arsenal and Whiteford Avenue, where she lived. In time, I was transferred to Georgetown University, then to Camp Ritchie in Western Maryland, then to Fort DuPont in Delaware, and Baltimore was within easy hitchhiking range of them all."

For millions of Americans, buying war bonds (known before Pearl Harbor as defense bonds) was a way of going to war without leaving home. The bonds were created by the federal government to finance the war. There may have been ways of getting rich during the war, but buying war bonds was not one of them; they paid 2.9 percent annual return after a ten-year maturity.

The promotion of war bonds may go down in history as the greatest, most spectacularly successful advertising campaign of all time. Promoters used every technique known to the media and entertainment world of those years. Their theme was simple, appealing, compelling, irresistible: buy war bonds because it is the patriotic thing to do; if you can't pick up a rifle, open your wallet.

Every day, in Baltimore and in every town and city across America, there was a war bond rally, big or small. The small rallies were held in places of employment and in schools and service clubs, churches, and synagogues, and with Boy Scout and Girl Scout troops. The big rallies, some monstrous, could be seen on stage, on the movie screen, in newspapers and magazines and be heard on the radio—with messages by the celebrities urging purchase of the bonds. Many rallies opened with a group singing "Any Bonds Today?" written by Irving Berlin, and closed with celebrity Kate Smith singing "God Bless America" (also written by

Irving Berlin). According to *NW Travel Magazine,* by the end of the war more than 85 million Americans, as much as half the population, had purchased war bonds, totaling $185.7 billion.

In those billions were counted the war bonds bought by these employees of Commercial Credit in Baltimore, on the night of December 17, 1941.

★ ★ ★ MOBILIZATION

The Japanese bombing of Pearl Harbor caught Baltimore off guard, but its response was immediate: Young men swamped the recruiting stations. Businesses and civilians sold war bonds. City fathers rushed to open USOs. Frenetic and overcrowded, life in the city, both work and play, went on, but post-Pearl Harbor mobilization meant that fathers, sons and daughters, friends and loved ones were volunteering or being drafted into the service. And so, while servicemen and servicewomen from all over America were flooding into the city, many Baltimoreans themselves were leaving it—for training somewhere, eventually for front-line duty in Europe or the Pacific. There was a quiet understanding that some would not come home.

"Something terrible has happened!"

Sunday mornings in Baltimore in 1941 were quiet and uneventful, a standard that Baltimore's earlier blue laws had established. They prohibited many stores from being open and proscribed some forms of Sunday recreation—all part of a civic struggle to better preserve the religious Sabbath. Aside from church services, not much was happening. Baltimoreans not in church spent the morning reading the Sunday papers and listening to the radio. Everybody had a radio.

It was over the radio that the news first broke, Sunday, early in the afternoon on December 7: "Japan bombs Pearl Harbor." The news left some in disbelief, others depressed, and still others with a vague sense that it was all too far away to worry about. But in the end, though Baltimoreans were hearing the news on a peaceful Sunday afternoon, they knew war when they heard it.

They heard it on one of about six radio stations (depending on the power of your set): WCBM, 680 on the dial, was offering "Radio City Music Hall"; WFBR, 1300, "Your Local News"; WBAL, 1090, "Modern Moods"—interviews with the Baltimore pundit Gerald Johnson; WITH, 1230, "Let's Hear Music"; WOR, 716, "News (from New York City)," leading into the Dodgers versus Giants professional football game. Most people probably heard the news on WCAO, then the local outlet for the Columbia Broadcasting System, delivered by the familiar voices of George Fielding Elliott, Elmer Davis, William L. Shirer, and Edward R. Murrow.

On that Sunday, early into the afternoon, Mildred Keiser, age seventeen, was off on her usual Sunday afternoon drive with her boyfriend, Mitchell Dubow. She recalled, "We were driving through Druid Hill Park, and the radio was on—and we heard. Our mood changed. Mitchell turned around and took me home. We knew."

At the same time, a few miles away, thirteen-year-old Robert "Bob" Rappaport was sitting in the sun parlor of his house at 4 Ellenham Road in Ruxton, fooling around with the family's new purchase, a state-of-the-art, all-in-one radio-phonograph. The radio offered the usual AM stations, and something new—"FM" stations, and an FM dial, though at the time there were few FM stations. With lots of fiddling around, Baltimoreans could pick up one FM station, two at the most. On that Sunday, just after noon, Bob was dialing back and forth and suddenly hit a sweet spot; between squeaks and squawks he heard: "We interrupt this program to bring you a special announcement." Bewildered and frightened, he ran into the living room, where his father and mother were sitting and reading the Sunday papers. He shouted, "Something terrible has happened! Something terrible has happened!"

That same Sunday afternoon, John Kopper, a twenty-nine-year-old electrical-engineering graduate student at Johns Hopkins, was working alone in the laboratory in Maryland Hall on the Homewood campus. He had no radio and neither saw nor spoke to anyone through the late morning and into the afternoon. It wasn't until he had left the lab and got to where he was living with his family, at 2718 St. Paul Street, at about 4:30 in the afternoon, that he found himself caught up in the news.

Hy Pusin was a twenty-seven-year-old aeronautical engineer living in Ashburton and working for the Glenn L. Martin Company, out for a Sunday drive with his wife in his 1933 Buick, when he heard the news on the car radio. He recalled, "I was alarmed, perhaps more than many, because the work I was doing was quite secret. I looked around immediately for a telephone booth along the road, but couldn't find one, so we turned around and went home. I called the security office of Glenn Martin. I wanted to know how the war would change things for me. They told me. Considerably.

"Within the hour, I arrived at the plant and found myself driving onto the parking lot under a net that had not been there the day before and that provided camouflage coloring over the entire lot. The camouflage was designed to look like landscape—browns, grays, and greens."

Eighteen-year-old Maurice "Chick" Paper, along with friends Edward "Eddie" Snyder and Norman Land, had just come out of the locker room of the Jewish Educational Alliance on East Baltimore Street at Central Avenue—they had been playing basketball in the gym. As was their habit every Sunday, after their game they walked a few blocks over to East Lombard Street and stopped into Attman's deli for their usual hot dog with mustard and homemade pickle. They had barely started to eat when they heard newsboys outside shouting: "Extra! Extra! Read all about it! Japan bombs Pearl Harbor!"

"Chick" Paper recalled, "I looked at Eddie and he looked at Norman and Norman looked at both of us, and we all asked each other the same question: 'Where's Pearl Harbor?'"

Not everybody felt restrained by the bad news. Movies proved to be more popular in war than they had been in peace. Even that Sunday night, good size crowds had gathered at the Hippodrome to see *The Men in Her Life,* featuring Loretta Young, and, on stage, the Milt Herth Trio; at the Stanley, *The Maltese Falcon,* with Humphrey Bogart and Mary Astor; and at the Century, Gene Tierney in *Sundown.*

Robert Rappaport, whose family owned the Hippodrome, explained the swollen attendance at the movies in wartime—that night and almost every day, too. "Workers had been pouring into Baltimore from Appalachia to work in the shipyards and aircraft factories in the build-up to the war. They suddenly had more money than they knew what to do with. Many worked the night shifts, and their free time was during the day, so every morning by ten the lines in front of the Hippodrome wound around the block. I remember the bedlam— every day, every night.

"But we knew we were at war, all right. Every Sunday morning, a few hours before the vaudeville show started, the performers would travel to a nearby USO or to Fort Meade or Fort Holabird in a couple of cars, to entertain the soldiers. One morning we sent the entire Charlie Spivak band and his vocalist, Connee Boswell—she was in a wheelchair—to Fort Meade. The performers would always be back in time for their regular show at 2:30."

John Kopper recalled, "Many people worked two jobs. They'd work a shift at one place, a second shift at another, then go to wherever they were boarding, change clothes and go downtown to the movies. I don't know when they slept."

Early intimations of war came in a predictable way at an unpredictable time, in the still-dark of that next Monday morning, December 8, 1941. Lines began forming shortly after midnight at the recruitment stations, though they were not scheduled to open until 9:00 a.m. By dawn, hundreds were milling about the entrance to the Main Post Office, at Calvert and Fayette streets. A recruitment officer there would tell a *Baltimore Afro-American* newspaper reporter, "We are in great need of all the men we can get, but we can use colored boys only as mess men." On the thirteenth the *Afro-American* reported the remark and then stated bluntly, "We cannot defend America with a dust brush, a mop and a white apron. Take down the color bar."

On that same Monday morning at about nine o'clock, a young Bob Rappaport arrived at Park School (then on Liberty Heights at Druid Park Drive), and within a few minutes learned that all classes had been dismissed. "We were ushered into the auditorium to hear, on the radio, President Roosevelt ask Congress to declare war on Japan." Most Baltimoreans, at work and at home or in school, heard that now-famous demand for a declaration of war crackling on their radios, but many walking about downtown in the heart of Baltimore's commercial and retail district learned of it, even as the *Sun* itself was receiving it, by staring up at the *Sun*'s electric news sign, the Trans Lux. The ominous words in lights in letters more than a foot high moved across a screen above the main entrance to the *Sun* building, on the southwest corner of Baltimore and Charles streets. The news read, "U.S. DECLARES WAR, 1,500 KILLED IN HAWAII."

So popular was the Trans Lux sign at Baltimore and Charles that the *Sun* placed one in Highlandtown and another at North Avenue

Rules published on Wednesday, December 10, three days after the attack on Pearl Harbor, provided instructions for what to do in the event of an air raid. Among them: "Fill the bathtub up with water...in case the water main breaks"; "If an incendiary bomb falls—play a spray from a garden hose on the bomb"; and "The air-raid alert signal here will be a rising and falling pitch or a series of short blasts for about five minutes."

and Charles. That same popularity inspired Baltimore poet Amy Greif to write in the *Sun:*

> Agape we read you dire and graphic
> There in the midst of thundering traffic
> We see the world's no field of clover
> No wonder if we get run over!

Among Baltimoreans driving in their cars and riding streetcars to and from work that morning, the mood was dark; the news was bad. With each bulletin the extent of wreckage from the attack on Pearl Harbor appeared more alarming; the fleet had been devastated. The Japanese were on the march in the South and Central Pacific.

On the evening of December 8, along with war news, readers of the *Sun* were confronted by this irony: Gilbert and Sullivan's *Mikado,* the classic spoof of Japanese manners and morals, was playing at Ford's Theater (Fayette and Eutaw) that evening. *Sun* critic Donald Kirkley would report, "The audience was quite small and not as demonstrative as Mikado audiences usually are. The reason may be simply the inability to disassociate the Japanese setting from today's newspaper headlines." That conclusion would appear to be reasonable, considering that while the lead character in the operetta, Nanki-Poo, was proclaiming, plaintively, that he was but a mere "wandering minstrel," thousands of Japanese soldiers were striking Malaya and Hong Kong, Guam, Wake and Midway. Before the show, John Little, the manager of Ford's, came stage front to assure the wary audience, "About the show tonight, it's all in fun." Subsequent reports suggested that few there were having any.

That same night, Jews from the village of Kolo, near Rastenberg, Poland, were being taken by vans to Chelmno, a village nearby. The next day, in groups, they were driven to a clearing in a wooded area. By the time the group arrived, they were dead, gassed by exhaust fumes funneled back into the van.

We had more Japs than we could handle

At about the same time Japanese aircraft were bombing Pearl Harbor, Japanese ships attacked tiny but strategically important Wake Island in the Central Pacific, two thousand miles west of Hawaii. The island's defense, now the stuff of legend, was led by a marine major, James Patrick Sinnott Devereux, of Ruxton, Maryland.

Years later in their retellings, the marines with Major Devereux would recall slightly different versions of their story, but they all mentioned waiting for Devereux to give the order to commence firing. The Japanese had begun to bombard the island when its fleet was still eight thousand yards off shore. Leroy N. Schneider, then a twenty-year-old private, was among the defenders there that long-ago afternoon. According to an account in the *Sun* (August 6, 1988), he said, "I thought, this guy is crazy. But then I realized that he knew what he was doing. The major finally gave the order to fire when the enemy was only four thousand yards away. For the Japanese, all hell broke loose." Mr. Schneider recalled that he and his men sank a Japanese destroyer, hit two cruisers, and damaged several other ships and that "thousands of Japanese were killed that day." After the war some Japanese historians confirmed Private Schneider's estimate of the American-inflicted damage and went one step beyond: Wake Island's defenders had dealt the Japanese one of their most humiliating defeats of the entire war.

Enemy aliens in Baltimore faced a directive from the U.S. attorney general: Surrender guns, cameras, binoculars, and shortwave radios to police for the duration of the war. Here, a plainclothes officer checks in some of the hundreds of items already received at police headquarters. In forty-eight hours, more than two hundred German and Italian citizens, and one from Japan, surrendered some three hundred articles. The deadline for surrender was midnight January 5, 1942.

In a second assault on December 23, the island fell. Major Devereux and his men were taken prisoner.

Somewhere in the middle of that battle, history gave way to myth. The story came out, and made its way around the world, that during a lull in the action a U.S. officer at Pearl Harbor asked Devereux if he needed help and that he snapped back, "Send us more Japs!" Back home, the message was electrifying; it heartened Americans demoralized by the earlier disaster at Pearl Harbor. It made for a great war story—only it wasn't true.

Its origins lay in the way an anonymous radio clerk on Wake Island crafted a coded message from Wake's overall commander, Navy

Cdr. Winfield Scott Cunningham, to Pearl Harbor. In an attempt to make decoding by the Japanese difficult, he wrote, "Send us stop now is the time for all good men to come to the aid of their party stop more Japs." From that scrambling of words designed to confuse any listening enemy came the popular interpretation, "Send us more Japs."

By the end of the war Major Devereux had become Lieutenant General Devereux and a folk hero. When he came home in October 1945, Baltimoreans gave him a parade through downtown, and a crowd of seventy-five thousand showed up to cheer him. By then he had disavowed the famous war cry of Wake Island: "We had more Japs than we could handle!"

The many worlds of wartime Baltimore

In the weeks following the outbreak of war and leading into the Christmas season, the downtown crowds, as they had in all the years within memory, gathered through the afternoon and into the evening, along the west side of Howard Street between Clay and Lexington streets to take in the Hochschild Kohn's and Hutzler's department stores' Christmas display windows.

Each of the windows, perhaps as many as ten or twelve, was a story high and a showpiece of ingenuity and complexity, light and movement, still life and animation. Inside the brightly lit sugar-plum miniature world, intricate self-contained scenarios were unfolding: a train chugged into a station and workmen began unloading it; a farmer milked his cows; firemen climbed and descended ladders; angels hovered like hummingbirds above a manger; children sledded down a snow-covered hill. It was a visual feast of color and joy. But it was more—it was a metaphor for wartime Baltimore.

Within any one window many scenarios were being played out, but none had anything to do with the others. The farmer milking his cows was disconnected from the children sledding down the hill; the freight car was being unloaded onto an earth far from the angels' heaven. And so it was in wartime Baltimore; though many and different scenarios were being played out against the backdrop of the war, each was at a remove from the other: The life of debutante society in Guilford went on, alongside but not connected to life in the working-class blocks of East Baltimore. While the air-raid spotters, staring out at the lonely skies, did their work silently, the crowds at Oriole Park were cheering lustily.

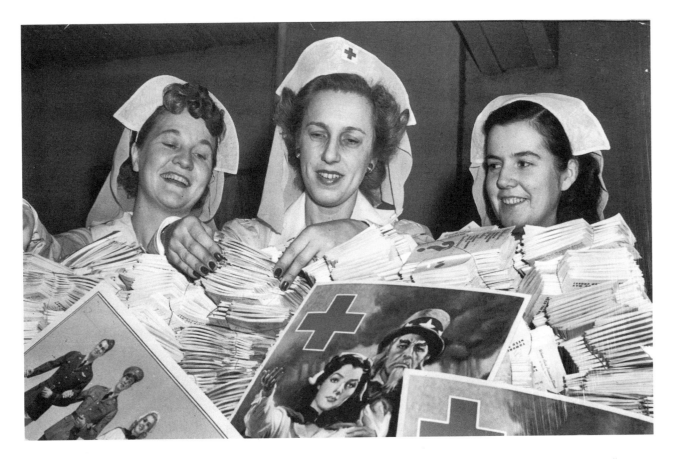

Days at the Red Cross headquarters were busy, with regular duties as well as recruitment campaign activities. On January 7, 1942, volunteers Mrs. Clinton Carr and Mrs. Irving B. Weinberg and staff assistant Mrs. W. H. Hartford sort campaign leaflets.

So there was not a "Home Front, Baltimore," there were "Home Fronts." Some people suffered a lot from the war; some not at all. Some profited from it, others were destroyed by it—all in the same city, all in the same war. Life in wartime Baltimore could be said to be Hochschild Kohn's and Hutzler's Christmas windows come to life, writ large.

"For a few weeks following Pearl Harbor," John Kopper recalled, "life didn't seem to change at all. Then one day I came back to my lab in Maryland Hall on the Johns Hopkins campus after lunch and was confronted by a soldier. He was armed, and blocking the door. He refused to let me in. I explained who I was and what I was doing, but he said, 'Sorry, we have a rumor that this building is scheduled to be blown up.'" After some tense conversation, an officer was called to the scene, and following a heated exchange, the soldier relented and John Kopper was admitted back into his lab. Life had changed, after all.

"A serious change would affect my life and make a huge difference in the way that those of us who were doing secret work in war-related

Among the first of many examples of youthful enthusiasm for the war effort—it fired emotions, and it could get you out of class!—Mary Stricker, student council president of Western High School (then on Gwynns Falls Parkway), proudly poses in mid-January 1942, with a first-aid belt she made herself.

industries would live our lives," Hy Pusin remembered. "We found ourselves uncomfortable in social situations because we had a fear that somehow we would unintentionally convey information about the work we were doing, and so our social life was limited. Wives in certain types of war-related work were not permitted to talk to their husbands about it. Husbands could not talk to their wives about it. There was this terrible need for secrecy. Fear touched our lives.

"About the only recreation I got was with friends who worked with me at Glenn Martin. We golfed regularly at Mount Pleasant. We worked five days straight, even through weekends, then got a day off—it might be a Monday or a Thursday. To some it seemed strange that during the war we were out golfing in the middle of the week, but that is the way things in Baltimore worked in wartime."

Gold stars in recognition of a family member killed in the war began to appear in windows of homes and businesses, but there were, at the same time, the great escapes—movies, wrestling matches at Carlin's Park and the Coliseum, concerts at the Lyric, dances at the Alcazar ballroom, cruises down the river. For some, for a precious few hours, the war could be far away.

Always in the background, around the clock, seven days a week, was the grim humming of Baltimore's huge complex of war produc-

On the morning of January 20, the girls at Western High School cheerfully and in the spirit of the event held an air-raid drill. At the same time the *Sun* decided to find out what life was like in Baltimore. The survey showed: insurance salesman Robert P. Albert was enrolled in a civilian defense organization; waitress Fanny Wilson said she was staying faithful to her soldier boyfriend in the Canal Zone, so no dates for her; salesman Lou Alexander was an air-raid warden; attorney Joe Kolodny said he was busier than ever dealing with clients' wartime taxes; telephone operator Elizabeth Wright signed up for the USO dances at Aberdeen Proving Ground and Fort Meade (she said, "War and the draft have made it tough getting dates"); cement salesman Cecil Branner said, "Now we use the car sparingly. No more Sunday drives"; elevator operator Eleanor Pitkevitz said that there were so many defense workers on the streetcars she could no longer get a seat going to work and coming back home.

In early 1942, Baltimore's leading dairies—Cloverland, Western Maryland, and Koontz—announced that they would no longer deliver milk daily, and downtown department stores—Hutzler's, Hochschild's, Stewart's, and the May Company—said that they would eliminate home delivery of "minor" items. The U.S. Pacific Command announced that Singapore had surrendered. As the war got on, women's dresses got shorter; lipstick, rouge, and face powder came in fewer shades; and the Japanese began an all-out attack on New Guinea.

Two of the fifteen young women in the local Red Cross Motor Corps find out what's amiss under the hood. The corps transported blood donors to and from donor projects, carried instructors to and from classes, and performed a variety of useful services. According to the *Sun* on January 25, 1942, "Important air-raid duties have been assigned to these worker drivers."

tion plants and the rhythm of life they created—three shifts every twenty-four hours, altering habits of shopping and recreation. As the old year drew to a close, while people were doing their Christmas shopping, the Japanese landed on the Philippine island of Mindanao. On Christmas Eve, while families gathered to trim the tree, Gen. Douglas MacArthur left Manila for the island of Corregidor. On Christmas Day, while Baltimoreans were opening their Christmas gifts, Hong Kong surrendered. Within days, people would be dancing in the New Year in the Charles Room of the Belvedere Hotel to the music of Lang Thompson and at the Alcazar to the music of Joe Dowling—all at a time when Japanese troops were overwhelming Malaya. The management of the famous Rennert Hotel, at Liberty and Saratoga streets, announced that, though the storied old hotel would be torn down, the bar and its mirror would be removed and set up in the new "refreshment room" of Carlin's Iceland. On the other side of the world the Japanese were attacking Manila in the Philippines.

In January 1942, the National Symphony performed at the Lyric, and people who were there recall that they saw in the audience a lot of navy blue and army khaki. Watching, listening to the symphony (Hans Kindler conducting, Guiomar Novaes, soloist), they could not

Volunteers serving the Baltimore chapter of the American Red Cross observed life-and-limb-saving techniques in preparation for the city's being bombed from the skies or fired upon from the seas—from the Chesapeake Bay or the inner harbor! These first-aid classes were being held at the headquarters of the Baltimore Chapter of the American Red Cross, at 202 Guilford Avenue, on January 27, 1942. Mrs. Adele Hoffman was teaching, and the members were learning specifically to apply "fixed traction" for fracture casts. Mrs. Raymond Scarlett is the "victim," and Mrs. Birdie Goodman is assisting, aided by J. F. Cooper.

know that at the very same time, savage fighting was raging in the Philippines, and Japanese troops were storming the beaches in the Solomon Islands.

The war had not yet changed the home front very seriously. It soon would.

In January news reached Baltimore that, many time zones away, Japanese troops had begun landing in New Guinea and that the first American troops who would fight in Europe were landing in Ulster, Northern Ireland. The public did not know that a joint U.S.-British planning committee, looking ahead to the invasion, then envisioned the need for a massive American force of one hundred five thousand—three infantry divisions and one armored division. German officials, led by Heinrich Heydrich, then sat around a table in the Berlin suburb of Wannsee discussing coolly what they called the "Final Solution" to the Jewish problem.

Wartime Baltimore was defined by sights and also by sounds. This air-raid siren, sometimes referred to as a "steam siren," seen here on the corner of Baltimore and St. Paul streets on Friday, February 20, 1942, is among the many air-raid sirens that were placed throughout the area. The screech of the air-raid siren made lasting impressions.

Air-raid training and race relations

Air-raid wardens checked on preparations for attack from the air: sand buckets in place? hose connected to the basement spigot? shelter room in the cellar set up for long hours of living on those nights when air-raid drills were scheduled? windows curtained, with no light showing? Lighted coastal cities obviously made easy targets for enemy planes or German submarines. German U-boats were in fact sinking merchant ships off the coast of Ocean City, Maryland.

Early in the new year, the city stirred up a hornet's nest when it announced a program to train citizens as air-raid wardens, with instructions to follow the pattern of racially segregated schools. Mayor Howard W. Jackson immediately acknowledged the charge of racial prejudice and apologized for it. The *Afro-American* ably reported the story on January 31:

"Mayor Howard W. Jackson admitted that the assigning of pro-

If you happened to be in your car when spotters in Delaware thought they had detected German bombers approaching the coastline of Ocean City, the Baltimore Civil Defense was there to save you! Its plan included these signs along the roadside, instructing you to stop, pull over to the right, put out your lights, and watch the CD volunteer standing in the road holding a flag with a CD imprint lowered at a right angle—confirming that there was an air-raid alert in progress—bringing traffic to a complete stop and so clearing the road for emergency vehicles! Got it? At the all clear (the Luftwaffe had been downed or turned back from Annapolis), the CD volunteer "removed" (as the sign inelegantly put it) the CD emblem from the scene, and you then were allowed to go on your way. As far as is known, such well-planned and well-intentioned efforts were exercises that made for lighthearted dinner-table conversation. No bombs fell.

spective air-raid wardens to classes in certain schools because of the color of the warden was un-American, un-Christian and wrong.

"The mayor's admission, plus the statement that he had taken up the question of separate classes for white and colored civilian defense volunteers with George Carter, chairman of the Baltimore Civil Defense Committee, was contained in a reply to a letter from Carl Murphy, editor of the AFRO and a member of the committee.

"Mr. Murphy's letter had reference to a complaint from Mrs. Josephine Williams of 426 N. Pine Street, who reported that she was refused admission to a class at school No. 1, Fayette and Greene Streets, after being originally assigned to that school by defense committee officials.

"Mr. Murphy's letter to Mrs. Williams, a copy of which was sent to the mayor, read in part: 'There is no reasonable argument that ex-

By February of 1942, just weeks after the United States had gone to war, Baltimore's downtown fortified itself. Preparations were everywhere to be seen. These sandbags, stacked against the windows of the Baltimore and Ohio Railroad Annex building at Lombard and Liberty, anticipated German air attacks.

plains the undemocratic method of assigning individuals to war-time instruction classes according to their color. I do not defend it and cannot. It is un-American, un-Christian and wrong. I hope, however, that you will not permit this to interfere with your patriotic duties for this reason: If this war lasts long enough, our white fellow citizens will learn to put aside their intolerance and accept all Americans as citizens. None of us who volunteer for public service will have to put up with insults as you have.'

"The Mayor's reply to Mr. Murphy was: 'I agree with you. I have taken the matter up with Mr. Carter and understand everything has been satisfactorily adjusted.'"

Jim Gentry's "Baltimore Red"

Sixty minutes out of every hour, twenty-four hours a day, starting December 8, 1941, and continuing through the duration of World War II, a corps of volunteers kept a lonely vigil, watching the skies over Baltimore. They were there to sound those two action-charged words, *Baltimore Red,* the signal that Baltimore was about to be attacked by enemy aircraft. The watchers were trained to recognize from textbook silhouettes the difference between friendly and enemy aircraft.

Hour after hour and day after day, the spotters would peer through field glasses, looking to see the dreaded silhouette and then to breathlessly pass the word, something like, "Luftwaffe at one o'clock, northwest to southwest at two thousand feet."

To young James "Jim" Gentry, it seemed as if the occasion would

On February 21, 1942, women applied for work at a Civil Defense office. Here, Mrs. Albert Stone is being interviewed for a position by Mrs. Virginia Goodman. In line and waiting, *left to right:* Mrs. A. B. Alexander, Ruth Grafton, Ellen Lauden, and Mrs. Thelma Johnson. Signs above on the wall provide reminders to the workers of their job responsibilities: "Be calm, Be cool, Prevent Panic," "Know Your People," "Make a Map, Know Your District!"

Air wardens blacked out this car at Thirty-third street and Greenmount Avenue—they sat on the lights.

A filling station goes dark at Thirty-third and Barclay.

"Pull up to the curb"—a policeman goes into action on the York road as the sirens sound.

According to the *Sun* on February 28, 1942, army observers classified a fifteen-minute Baltimore blackout between 9:45 and 10:00 the previous night as "Perfect. Best in U.S." Even so, there had been more than three hundred violations.

The proprietors of a bowling alley had refused to turn out the inside lights—perhaps for safety reasons, given the mix of beer and bowling balls—but also the neon sign on the exterior. A warrant was sworn out. Residents of at least ten houses in northeast Baltimore, defying requests from the air-raid wardens, flatly refused to turn out the lights inside their homes.

Air-raid wardens had their troubles with automobiles parked with lights burning and owners nowhere around. Four wardens spotted a car at Greenmount and Thirty-third and learned from persons nearby that the owner had gone to the movies, leaving on headlights and taillights. The wardens thought of smashing the lights but instead simply sat on them until the all clear sounded. They then called a policeman, who ticketed the car for a blackout violation.

A policeman and several wardens were confronted with a similar problem at Castle and Monument, where another parked car was found—locked, and with all lights burning. Among the options open to them, the wardens chose one not used before: they saw some cardboard boxes nearby and cut pieces to place over the lights. The technique worked—and when the driver returned he found not only cardboard draped over his headlights but also a ticket tucked under his windshield wiper.

Meantime, an air-raid warden posted atop Public School #5 at Westerwald Avenue and Thirty-fifth Street reported sighting a swastika about three feet square painted on the roof of a house on nearby Melville Avenue. Not only that, but every light in the house was on. The warden called the Northeastern District police.

For comic relief, there was this, in the Larchmont section of Baltimore County. The neighborhood was a model of compliance with the exception of one lone light emanating from the bedroom of an apartment dweller. A warden banged on the door in an effort to talk face to face with the occupant and get the light doused. The resident, hearing the commotion and determined to find out what it was all about, switched on the porch light. Some wardens had no luck.

A lovely footnote to the historic blackout entered the world at 9:50 p.m., five minutes after the lights had gone out—a seven-pound baby girl born at Volunteers of America Hospital to Mrs. Howard Shipley, of 808 South Fagley Street. The parents said they had not yet decided on a name. The hospital staff called her "Blackie."

On March 8, 1942, children at P.S. 211 elementary school at Belair Road and Frankford Avenue found themselves practicing for an air raid. "When the alarm rings," the paper reported, "each child is to get his or her coat, take it to the shelter, and sit on it." Fortunately, the bombs never fell.

never come. Jim, who as a boy accompanied his father on cold Saturday mornings to take the dawn watch, recalled, "We'd go over to the American Legion spotting tower on the Mount Pleasant golf course, and through our field glasses, search out the skies—which were always empty."

But as winter deepened in 1942, at another tower, a spotter thought he did see a squadron of German bombers bearing down on the sleeping city. Keeping calm as he was trained to do, he spoke carefully in to his headset, "Luftwaffe, flying due south at two o'clock." Within seconds the dreaded word was flashed to the spotting towers from North Carolina to Maine. An alerted army defense headquarters begged the Baltimore spotter for more information, at which point the spotter seemed to hesitate. An awkward silence followed. Finally, the (unidentified) spotter said, "Hold it a minute. Those planes are flapping their wings. Uh-uh. Cancel. We hear them honking. Sound the all clear." They did, marking the day in World War II when Baltimore was spared from being driven into its air-raid shelters by a flock of flapping, honking geese heading south.

★ Indicates Regulation USO Club Building
● Indicates Other USO Units and Operation

The Spirit of '42

In three words, the marines on Wake Island summed up the spirit that is being shown by American forces in every action of the present conflict.

Facing impossible odds, those marines' only reply, when asked if they wanted anything sent them, was:

"Yes . . . More Japs."

That reply notified the whole world that the old American verve and snap—the will to fight and keep on fighting—was still there and hitting on all cylinders.

It reflected the sort of spirit that our men have shown not only at Wake Island, but also in the Philippines . . . in Macassar Straits . . . at the Gilbert and Marshall Islands . . . wherever they have met the enemy.

Our men's knowledge that a united nation backs them up—that "the people back home" appreciate and care for them—certainly has something to do with this spirit.

The hospitality, comforts, conveniences, social and recreational activities we provide for them while they are at liberty or on leave among us, therefore, have important repercussions on the enemy engaging our men.

To help provide such aids and services for our men, six great voluntary service agencies of the country—the Young Men's Christian Association, the Salvation Army, the Jewish Welfare Board, the National Catholic Community Service, the Young Women's Christian Association, and the Travelers Aid Society—last year banded together at the request of the Government to form the United Service Organizations and carry on a great organized program for sustaining and strengthening the morale of all our men in uniform.

Baltimoreans found themselves walking on sidewalks, traveling streets, attending movies, and visiting restaurants more crowded than they had ever seen them. Newcomers from the hinterlands continued to come for work at defense plants; the numbers of soldiers, sailors, and airmen stationed in Baltimore or at nearby installations only increased after Pearl Harbor, and they thronged to town for diversion and pleasure. Responding, Baltimore's civic leadership in the spring of 1942 established six United Service Organizations (everyone referred to them as "USOs"). The first opened in mid-March, at 339 North Charles, formerly a large store, Dulany-Vernay's.

Overall, the operating agencies consisted of the Young Men's Christian Association, Young Women's Christian Association, Salvation Army, Jewish Welfare Board, National Catholic Community Services, Traveler's Aid Society, and "Colored" branches of the YMCA and YWCA. The establishment on Charles Street, run by the Catholic community leadership, adopted an "open-house attitude," according to the *Sun's* account of the opening. "My idea," said club director George Woodson Proffitt, "is to get away from any sort of regimentation of the boys. They won't have to do anything they don't want to. They can read, play games, do just what they like." Here servicemen—besides dancing in a large second-floor ballroom and eating heartily—could play pool, Ping-Pong, and shuffleboard; bowl; swim in the pool; dabble in photography; browse in a large library, thanks to generous response to the Victory Book Campaign; write letters; listen to the radio; or build model airplanes in a hobby room. The basement included a recording booth, where a soldier could talk a letter into a machine that would cut a record to send home. The third and fourth floors featured showers and bunks enough to accommodate nearly three hundred men.

Opening ceremonies had run to the extravagant. Besides greetings from Mayor Howard W. Jackson, a major who served as "morale officer" for the Third Corps Area Service Command (which included Baltimore), and Cleveland R. Bealmear, USO Council chair for the city, planners staged a "Miss Columbia and her court" pageant in which "Miss Elizabeth White, a model," rallied around her women, who supposedly had grown up in or had a tie to every state in the Union, "selected from the female ranks of local social security workers, accompanied by servicemen in uniform." At the climax of this event, Gov. Herbert R. O'Conor crowned Miss Liberty and made a short address. Dinner and dancing followed.

In the March 1942 issue of the *Councillor,* a national magazine for USO leadership, Grace Hooper Mc-Neal explained that the USO program in Baltimore then was "increasing rapidly." "The purpose," she said, "was to organize and carry on a program for sustaining and strengthening the morale of our young men in uniform, and, too, of our men and girls in the factories who constitute that group called 'the man behind the man behind the gun.'"

Authorities passed out this map to service personnel bound for Baltimore. It recommended that servicemen and women visit the USO at 339 North Charles, the YMCA at 24 West Franklin, or the YWCA at 128 West Franklin. There also were the Young Men's and Young Women's Hebrew Associations, at 305 West Monument, in a building that had opened in 1930, the YWCA at 1200 Druid Hill Avenue, the YMCA at 1619 Druid Hill Avenue, and a new facility at Gold and Blunt streets.

Air Cadets get a big sendoff! In Baltimore the Benevolent and Protective Order of Elks became sponsors of aviation cadets, starting up bond funds for each cadet under the slogan, "You buy 'em, we'll fly 'em."

In late March, to music furnished by the thirty-two-piece Third Corps Area Service Command band, the cadets paraded through downtown, from the Equitable Building at Fayette and Calvert to the Elks Lodge no. 7, at 307 West Fayette. There each cadet received a defense bond savings book containing a $1 starter stamp. His sponsor, a lodge member, had committed to send his cadet a $1 defense stamp monthly until sponsor and cadet together had accumulated the equivalent of an $18.75 U.S. Savings Bond.

So the lads took off for training with a savings account. Cadets and sponsors planned to correspond with one another for the duration of the war.

As predicted, at about 9:30 in the morning of Saturday, March 28, 1942, it started to rain. By afternoon, to everyone's surprise, the rain began to be mixed with snow. But it was spring, and so Baltimoreans didn't give the unseasonably foul weather a second thought, and turned in for the night.

Not many Baltimoreans were still awake in the wee hours, when that rain began turning to solid, heavy snow. They awoke Sunday morning (a week past the start of spring) to what would prove to be, by the time it stopped at around ten o'clock that night, the heaviest March snowfall in the history of the city—somewhere between two and three feet. It was Palm Sunday.

With Easter a week away the city lay paralyzed. Phone and power lines had come crashing down under the enormous weight of the sodden snow. Streetcars were stopped on their tracks. Stores and municipal offices closed. Property damage was heavy. Palm Sunday church attendance turned out to be light.

Many people who can recall the snowfall say that most churches did not even open that morning. Weatherman John R. Weeks called the surprise storm, in the understatement of that decade, "a freak." He said it had not been anticipated by the U.S. Weather Bureau and was as much a surprise to him as it was to Baltimoreans. He said the ferocity of the storm and the timing of it gave families a lot to write about to their sons far away.

The *Sun* reported that "because of certain wartime restrictions the reporting of the storm was written and published in consultation with the Office of Censorship and the War Department."

Streetcars go to war! The United Railways and Electric Company, owners and operators of Baltimore streetcars and trackless trolleys, worked with government agencies to make their vehicles traveling billboards in support of the war. Included were cars painted "Women, Take War Work!" "On to Tokyo," "Serve 12 Hours Each Week in Uniform," "Women Needed Now!

Join the WAVES," and "Serve in the Armed Forces! U.S. Coast Guard Port Security Force. Apply 17 South Street." While the cars rolled, Japanese forces intensified their assault on the thousands of Americans and Filipinos trapped on Bataan. Forced to surrender to the Japanese on April 9, 1942, they were led on the sixty-five-mile march that became known as the

"Bataan Death March." That was the same week in Baltimore when popular performers Sophie Tucker and George Jessel opened at Ford's Theater in the Broadway-bound show *High Kickers. News-Post* critic Norman Clark pronounced it "a high-class burlesque show."

The audience set up an enthusiastic din, lasting for minutes

War workers and their needs changed a lot in Baltimore, even the town's moviegoing habits. A few minutes after midnight the morning of April 15, 1942, the first predawn movie was presented at the Century Theater on Lexington Street, in response to a petition by the day shift and swing shift (4:00 p.m. to midnight) workers of the Bethlehem-Fairfield shipyard. The petition called for a "midnight show" at the local theaters because, they claimed, their work schedules denied them the usual opportunity to go to the movies during normal hours. The performance drew two thousand workers to the first special trial run. The theater's manager, William Sexton, called it a "great success." "We've scheduled another after-midnight show for next Wednesday," he told the *Sun.* "If it does as well, we'll make early-morning showings a regular practice."

J. M. Willis, vice-president and general manager of the Bethlehem-Fairfield shipyard, attended the performance at 12:30 a.m. He talked with some of the war workers who attended and said that he was "very pleased," and the experiment showed that the workers really wanted and needed after-midnight recreation. "The workers came with their wives or girl friends. They made it a gala affair. They applauded much more than a normal movie audience.

"We learned one thing more from the showing. We found that the workers would like to have time to get home to clean up and dress before coming to the show. Next week, therefore, the feature picture won't begin at 1:00 a.m., as it did this morning, but a half hour or so later."

At the end of the feature picture, a Bethlehem-Fairfield executive went stage front to thank the workers for attending. Mr. Sexton said later, "No Hollywood star could have been given a better reception. The audience set up an enthusiastic din, lasting for minutes. I've never heard anything like it in my years in the business."

The Stanley Theater (Howard at Centre Street) was also planning after-midnight showings.

"Filter centers": Spotting enemy aircraft that weren't

Air-raid "filter centers" were now in operation "somewhere in Baltimore," doing their work silently and secretly in unidentified locations, although there were whisperings that some lay "deep below in certain downtown buildings." The centers received the communications passed along to them from the air-raid spotters, who were stationed in towers throughout the area. Trained personnel in the centers would then take the information, for example, that a plane had been sighted, and then, using long-handled pointers to push markers across a tabletop map, and taking into account a plane's course and speed, plot the plane's apparent destination—and worry about its business in the skies over Baltimore.

"My mother, at odd times of the day and night," Bob Rappaport recalled, "would disappear to some secret location where, I was told, she did 'war work' at a filter station. Sometimes she was not at home when I went to bed; sometimes she was not there when I woke. My father said, 'Your mother's doing war work at the filter center.'"

Mrs. Rappaport's secret work at a filter center in Baltimore coincided with secret work on the other side of the world. On April 18, a squadron of American B-25 bombers under the command of Lt. Col. James H. "Jimmy" Doolittle took off from the carrier USS *Hornet* and flew some eight hundred miles to the Japanese mainland. There, swelling American hearts with pride, they dropped their bombs on Tokyo before dispersing; many crew members were lost or captured. On that same day in Baltimore, Carlin's amusement park at Park Heights Avenue and Reisterstown Road announced its big news—the grand opening of the new summer season, and, to hype opening day, "Admission Free!"

Over There: The week of May 4, 1942, in the Coral Sea
Throughout the week, Baltimoreans were getting the news that in the Coral Sea, between Australia and the Solomon Islands in the South Pacific, the navies of Imperial Japan and the United States were locked in a fierce sea battle. Every day brought additional word of carrier strikes, sinkings, and casualties. It would turn out to be the battle that ended Japan's advance southward and westward, removing the threat to Australia.

Over Here: The week of May 4, 1942, at the Baltimore Zoo
Baltimoreans were getting the news that on Saturday (May 9) "Minnie the Elephant" would be performing: "Minnie, the new glamour girl at the Druid Hill Park Zoo," reported the *Sun* on May 10, "made a formal appearance yesterday afternoon before thousands of applauding friends who watched her act on the Mansion House lawn, and made it clear that she does not intend to let any person or anything steal her show. Like any temperamental prima donna, Minnie, the eight-year-old elephant who arrived here on Saturday to succeed the late lamented Mary Ann in the affections of Baltimore children—and many of its older folks—gave every indication that she intends to keep the spotlight on herself."

There was no band for Minnie to dance to, but she was not deterred. She stood on a box and played the harmonica, and following the George M. Cohan routine for bringing down the house at the end of the show, waved two American flags as the crowd gave her a big hand.

In the spring of 1942, Baltimoreans found themselves in a new and life-changing home front battle—rationing was making itself felt in day-to-day living. Everything you wanted or thought you wanted, or needed or thought you needed, became, suddenly, rationed or scarce: gasoline, tires, silk, typewriters, shoes, products made with rubber or nylon, and most all foodstuffs—including meat and sugar. The rules could be complex and bewildering, and figuring them out, living with them, became a way of life.

Regulations for sugar seemed to cause particular confusion: stamp no. 1 was good for the purchase of one pound of sugar only from May 6 to May 16; no. 2, for one pound of sugar from May 17 through May 30; no. 3,

for one pound of sugar from May 31 through June 13; no. 4, from June 13 through June 27. Grocers went to war with the Maryland Ration Board to make things clearer; some just gave up and pasted the notice up on bulletin boards for the customer to figure out.

On May 5, 1942, South Baltimore Grocer George Tabak *(pictured)* measured out a pound of sugar for Mrs. Roszel Thomsen, *fourth from left,* who presented her coupons. Waiting behind her, stamps at the ready, are, *left to right,* Mrs. Margaret Kirby, Mrs. Adeline Truckenmiller, Grace Cochran, Mrs. Kathryn Mostyn, and Mrs. Catherine Krach. Their mood seems cheerful, patient, accepting.

No one in Baltimore could know that in the spring of 1942 Jews in

Poland were being rounded up and deported to the newly opened concentration camp, Belzec, there to be gassed.

Must have 1942 registration

Something unusual was happening on Sunday, May 10, 1942, along Charles, Howard, St. Paul, Lombard, and Pratt streets—the main arteries that led motorists from one part of Baltimore to another. Cars were backed up in long lines, making for bumper-to-bumper traffic jams: everyone knew that this was the last Sunday for a pleasure drive. Gasoline rationing was going into effect the following Friday (May 15), and this fling was a last-minute attempt to enjoy one more Sunday drive, so much a part of a peacetime Baltimore. Before the week was out, the tradition would be history. The start of gasoline rationing came as no surprise. For weeks prior, Baltimoreans had heard about and debated it. The rules for rationing were by this time well known and digested:

There were five classes:

Class A

WHO GETS CLASS A—All persons who use their car for pleasure only, or who drive less than six miles a day in connection with their work.

CLASS A QUOTA—Class A ration cards have seven units. Each unit is good for three gallons of gasoline. Class A cards therefore, are good for a total of 21 gallons of gasoline anytime between May 15 and July 1.

Class B-1

WHO GETS CLASS B-1—All persons who drive an average of from six to ten miles a day *in carrying on their work or in commuting to and from their work.*

CLASS B-1 QUOTA—Class B-1 ration cards have eleven units. Each unit is good for three gallons of gasoline. Class B-1 cards, therefore, are good for a total of 33 gallons of gasoline between May 15 and July 1.

Class B-2

WHO GETS CLASS B-2—All persons who drive an average of from 10 to 14 miles per day *in carrying on their work or in commuting to and from their work.*

CLASS B-2 QUOTA—Class B-2 ration cards have 15 units. Each unit is good for three gallons of gasoline. Class B-2 cars therefore are good for a total of 45 gallons of gasoline between May 15 and July 1.

A joke in the spring of 1942 ran, "If you see a line of people, get in it." This one, at P.S. 85, Lakewood and Oliver on May 28, 1942, was for sugar-rationing cards.

Class B-3

WHO GETS CLASS B-3—All persons who drive an average of more than 14 miles a day *in carrying on their work or in commuting to and from their work.*

CLASS B-3 QUOTA—Class B-3 ration cards have 19 units. Each unit is good for three gallons. Class B-3 cards therefore are good for a total of 57 gallons of gasoline between May 15 and July 1.

Class X

WHO GETS CLASS X—Class X cards are reserved for ambulances, hearses, taxicabs, medical and nursing professions, trucks, official federal, state, and municipal cars and construction and repair vehicles rendering public service.

CLASS X QUOTA—X cards entitle the holder to unlimited quantities of gasoline.

Must Have 1942 Registration

All persons applying for a gasoline ration book must have their 1942 motor-vehicle registration card with them at the time of registration.

Motorists who use their auto in their work, or to drive to and

The No. 4 streetcar line was West Baltimore's link to the world beyond, serving Walbrook, Bloomingdale Road, Edmondson Avenue, and on to Saratoga Street and into the heart of downtown—linking to transfer points in every direction.

from work, and are therefore applying for a Class B card must be prepared to answer the following. If you drive to work, what is the shortest mileage from your home to your regular place of work? How many miles do you drive each working day in carrying on your work (other than from your home to work and back)? What is the total average daily mileage customarily driven in the car described to get to and from work and to carry on work?

In an editorial of May 11, the *Sun* worried that the rationing as structured would not work and warned that more drastic measures might be needed, but proclaimed it worthwhile:

"If every mile of frankly useless driving were eliminated, the new ration might not suffice. We are going to have to eliminate also a great deal of highly useful driving—marketing, serving household needs, taking children to school and many other journeys that are far from being pleasure trips. This will really hurt but the hardship will be borne and if the rationing keeps the workers moving it will be a success."

Over Memorial Day weekend—the first wartime Memorial Day weekend—almost every pump in the city went dry. Drivers, glancing furtively at fuel gauges, tried to find new sources. They seldom could. On Memorial Day itself, on Liberty Heights Avenue, drivers

Because of gas shortages, shoppers
had to be inventive in getting to and
from the grocery store. Mrs. Joseph
Villa and her daughter Rosalie appeared to have solved the problem—at
least for this one trip back from the
grocery store in early summer, 1942.

Gas ration card issued to Jack Louis Sollins, of 1523 North Appleton. Mr. Sollins had a grocery store on the corner of Baker and Poplar Grove, and he used his car, a 1941 Pontiac coupe, to deliver his orders. "He bought a coupe," his son, Leonard recalled, "because it had plenty of space in the back to hold the groceries he had to deliver."

Mr. Sollins was issued a Class B-3 card. He and his family lived only about eight blocks away, so getting to and from work did not pose an extra gas problem.

found only three pumps open between Garrison Boulevard and the city line, and these gas stations were limiting customers to three gallons each.

While Baltimoreans adjusted to the life-changing reality of gasoline rationing, which would in effect control their lives by controlling where and how much driving they could do, the Japanese and American fleets were in a battle for control of Midway Island; and on the Murmansk run to Russia, German aircraft were attacking and sinking Allied merchant ships loaded with war materiel. As the new gas rules went into place, filling stations had lines two and three blocks long.

Before shipping out in 1942, merchant seamen Clyde Hanor of Detroit, Michigan, and John McGee, of Tampa, Florida, manage to get in a game of pool at the USO at 339 North Charles.

Every day, seven days a week, hundreds of servicemen crowded the four floors of the Charles Street USO. On the first floor were a lounge, reception center, snack bar, soda fountain, game room, kitchen, and chow hall. But the ballroom on the second floor drew the most attention and proved to be the center of this USO world. It had a piano and stage at one end. According to the USO *Councillor* that March, the ballroom would "be used for entertainment purposes, as well as to encourage histrionic ability which may be latent, or otherwise, in our armed forces." Mostly the large room provided the space for churning young people to dance, either to live bands or the jukebox playing "jitterbug" music. Hostesses were carefully selected; they were pretty, friendly, and liked to dance. On some nights at the Charles Street USO servicemen numbered two hundred.

In 1942, nineteen-year-old Ruth Weitzman was an administrative assistant in the office of the USO located in the Young Men's and Young Women's Hebrew Association (YMHA and YWHA) building at 305 West Monument. "One day a young soldier came in the office," she recalled. "He told me that he was stationed at Aberdeen and was sent to this office to get prayer books for the Jewish soldiers to use in their religious services on Saturdays. He said he was Cpl. Jacob Hurwitz, and could I help him.

"I told him we had plenty of the prayer books he was looking for and

were only too happy to lend them to him. Every Monday he would return the books, and every Friday morning he would come back and ask for them again. But one day he asked for more than books. He asked for a date.

"Well, in those wartime days, the request was not so unusual. The soldiers were far from home and lonely and found themselves in a city where they knew no one. So I accepted. Lots of girls dated servicemen they met in the USOs. Corporal Hurwitz and I went out together several times. Of course, this being wartime, in no time we were in love. In wartime everything gets speeded up.

"Late in 1942 he was sent overseas to the China-India-Burma Theater, and we corresponded through the years he was away. He came home in 1946, and, yes, we got married. All because in 1942 he asked me for some prayer

books in the USO on Monument Street."

A heartening wartime incident took place in the spring of 1942, when, after being stationed at posts far apart, three brothers in the service who had not seen each other for almost a year reunited briefly at the Charles Street USO. The *Sun* reported on Sunday, May 11, that Thomas, Kenneth, and William Lang had arranged to meet there the night before and call home, which the paper could only locate as "somewhere in the Mid-West." Shortly after they arrived, the USO office wired their mother to be standing by to take the call from her three sons. The plan worked beautifully. Mrs. Lang got to talk to all three of her sons and at the same time—over long-distance telephone from a USO in Baltimore.

If the German bombers *were* to find Baltimore in the dark, it would not be the fault of Mrs. Elizabeth Gray, of 3707 West Belvedere Avenue, and young neighbors Nancy Lee Hoff, age eight, and Emma Jean Sawyer, age six, shown here in strict compliance with the rules for blacking out a home. Mrs. Gray is reading a magazine, and the children are doing their homework— all by candlelight.

This blackout, the night of June 3, 1942, was described the next day as both a success and a foretaste of more drastic tests of the city's defenses in the near future. Streetlights and traffic signals were left on, allowing automobiles and other vehicles to proceed normally, and certain war plants were excused, but the rest of the city was blacked out from 9:00 p.m. to midnight. Most of the violations reported were of minor chinks of light.

The blackout was one in a series planned by Baltimore's Civil Defense Corps. It was their observation that few households had made any serious preparations for extended blackouts. Last-minute catch-up purchases of blackout materials confirmed that the committee had it right.

John Kopper was an air-raid warden whose job was to police Maryland Hall on the Hopkins campus to look for blackout violations. "But I never saw any," he said. "I did notice that on Calvert Street there were gas lamps that had to be turned off, and I knew that the only way they *could* be was for somebody to get up to the height of each lamp on a ladder and pull a chain to turn each one of them off. Don't know how it was done but at blackout time, somehow or another, *all of those lamps seemed to go off at once.* Amazing."

Hy Pusin used brown wrapping paper to seal off the openings in the windows of his house in Ashburton, where light might come through. He said, "I never had the feeling that blackouts in Baltimore were taken very seriously, and neither did some city officials. We all cooperated, of course, but nobody I knew really believed that the city was ever in danger of being bombed. There was a lot of joking about it."

U.S. Navy recruiters made the six-month anniversary of Pearl Harbor an "Avenge Pearl Harbor" commemoration and folded it into Flag Week of 1942. On June 7, about seventy volunteers paraded through downtown like heroes, past the War Memorial Plaza, then to the row house in which Mary Pickersgill and her daughter had sewed the colors that later became the Star Spangled Banner. Then on Pratt Street, in the open air, the men and their families listened to heavy oratory before, mercifully, standing to swear the oath of allegiance and then rendering their first salute as sailor recruits. The *Sun* reported that a radio broadcast carried the ceremony from coast to coast and to "fighting men overseas."

Bethlehem Steel's Sparrows Point shipyard, along with the company's newly constructed yard on the site of an old Pullman Company plant in the city's Fairfield section, was jammed with work for the navy. The Bethlehem-Fairfield yard, which built and launched the first Liberty ship, the *Patrick Henry,* in 1941, hummed with activity around the clock.

Liberty ships were named for deceased prominent American men and women: presidents, governors, Supreme Court justices, actors, railroad presidents, aviators, musicians, industrialists, artists, writers, union leaders, newspaper barons, and signers of the Declaration of Independence. On this occasion, July 25, 1942, the yard launched the *John P. Poe*—

named after the lawyer and long-time political figure in Maryland's Democratic party. Later in the war, the Bethlehem-Fairfield yard provided the setting for the launch of the *John H. Murphy,* named for the founder of the *Afro-American* newspaper chain, and the *John W. Brown,* named for an aggressive labor organizer in the shipbuilding, mining, and carpentry industries, who had died in 1941. (The *Brown* herself served faithfully throughout the war and survived it—one of only two such Libertys still afloat. Restored, the *Brown* is tied up in her homeport of Baltimore.)

Within a year of the *Poe's* launching, the Bethlehem-Fairfield yard employed 46,700 workers, including 6,000 African Americans. By war's

end, they had constructed 384 Liberty ships, 94 Victory ships, and 30 LSTs (landing ship, tank) and claimed shipbuilding records. From the opening of the yard in 1941 until it launched its last ship, the *Atlantic City Victory,* on September 19, 1945, the facility delivered more vessels than any other American shipyard.

Top, "Don't fence me in...," "Lay that pistol down, Babe...," "I'll walk alone ..." Sing-a-longs were part of the entertainment provided by the USOs. Hostesses who could sing and smile could make a homesick soldier feel better about the world. On this late June night in 1942, Suzanne Kahn plays the piano.

Right, Bring 'em on! A group of Towson gentlemen decided to take matters of defense into their own hands. Rifles at the ready, they here pose at the Baltimore County Court House before an organizational meeting on the afternoon of June 25, 1942. The "Towson Minutemen" dared the Axis to invade Baltimore County.

Top, Ready for the real thing! During an early July 1942 drill, Civil Defense officials cut the power at the Southern District Headquarters. The men switched over to lanterns, the *Sun* reported, "with no interruption to their work."

Right, Passengers on this No. 15 streetcar got caught in a blackout on July 15, 1942. With their schedule upset, possibly making them late for work or home, they show traces of weariness, resignation, bewilderment, frustration, and very little merriment at what was at best an exercise. The No. 15 served East Baltimore, south on Belair Road onto Gay Street and all the way to Baltimore Street.

Finding themselves that summer of '42 settled in a bomb shelter for a stay of indeterminate length deep inside the Baltimore Gas and Electric building at Lexington and Liberty, these workers betray different moods. Most seem to be taking the drill in good spirits. Others appear worried, perhaps about missing work or getting somewhere late. In any case, the all clear always sounded eventually.

Not until July 15, 1942, seven months into the war, did Baltimore stage the first dusk-to-dawn blackout that it counted a success. "Several persons," according to the *Sun,* "failed to heed the warnings of wardens to get off the streets during the half-hour period when the blackout was total, with all the street lights extinguished and all automobiles, except essential vehicles such as fire apparatus and police and civil-defense cars, halted with lights out."

Officials noted that the main offenders were people who went out and left lights burning. Violations were reported to a central clearing office, to be studied "for appropriate action." Reports read, "Warrants will be sought."

"This is the Army, Mr. Jones,
No private rooms or telephones.
You had your breakfast in bed before,
But you won't have it there any more."

Among the hit songs of the wildly successful musical *This Is the Army* was "This Is the Army, Mr. Jones." In the summer of 1942, Hutzler's department store, using state-of-the-art marketing, tied itself into the show's popularity by staging an exhibit designed to attract the "*Mrs.* Joneses" of Baltimore into their store: "July 17 through July 29 . . . Second Floor, No Admission Charge." "Come to Hutzler's," advertisements beckoned, "to see how the Army cares for your boy and girl." On display: "This is a mine detector," "This is a handie talkie," "This is a field switchboard," and "This is a bazooka."

In November, *This Is the Army* reached Ford's Theater on Fayette Street.

There was no getting away from the war. The *Sun,* the *News-Post,* and the *Afro-American* newspapers, along with the radio stations (there was no television), provided continuous coverage. Even streetcars were painted up with signs that kept the citizenry reminded of war. And if you somehow missed all of that, there were posters everywhere—where you worked, shopped, dined—to stir patriotism ("Avenge Pearl Harbor"); to educate, as does the poster shown ("Comparative Sizes of Bombs" and their "Depth of Penetration"); to warn ("Sugar Hoarders Beware!"); and to solicit funding ("Buy Bonds!").

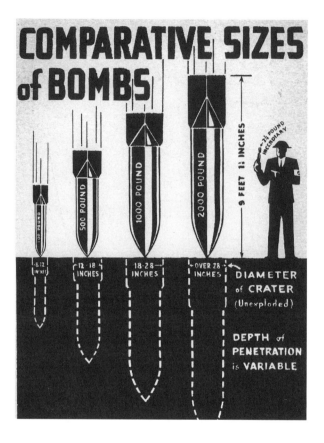

Never missed a day's work in the four years of the war

"My husband and I were living at 1103 St. Paul Street," remembers Louisa Reynolds. "I was thirty-one years old, and alone in the house when I heard the news on the radio, the Japanese had bombed Pearl Harbor! It was such a *shock!* My husband was out, working on our boat at the Maryland Yacht Club, when he heard the news, and he rushed home. We knew war was imminent, but still, we were truly shocked at the news.

"Within days I was working downtown for the Red Cross, somewhere in the Mount Vernon area, I believe. I worked there six days a week through to the end of the war. I learned to take blood. I always wanted to give them my own blood but they never would take it. Never missed a day's work in the four years of the war. We were taught what to do about casualties, should we be attacked. My teacher was Mrs. Haussner of the restaurant Haussner's. She was a demon, but she made the hard work exciting.

"To me rationing, *rationing,* was among the most discomforting problems of wartime in Baltimore. That, and the blackouts. I remem-

In its quest to acquire scrap for conversion into war materiel (in this case, rubber), the military obviously did not care where the community chose to accumulate the bounty. This site, for example, is in downtown Baltimore at Calvert and Fayette, in the very heart of the heavily trafficked legal/financial center of those years, in the small park that is home to the Battle Monument. This view looks east, from the city courthouse to the post office and federal courthouse, on July 30, 1942. Margaret Frederick tosses a rubber inner tube onto the pile, and a few feet away, Betty Elliott makes her contribution—a bicycle tire.

Not everyone with an old tire threw it onto this or one of the many other piles in scrap rubber-collection stations around town. Some people, in a time when new tires were difficult and sometimes impossible to buy, took their old tires in for what was commonly known as a "retreading," a process that called for affixing a fairly thin new tread to a tire on which the original tread had worn thin or was gone altogether.

ber those ration books—everything seemed to be rationed. Coffee, and tea in particular, seemed hard to get. I'd stand in a line in Lexington Market to get a roast—once in a while we could get beef or pork. Chicken was easy to get, because, I guess, we raised a lot of them locally. You had to have a good relationship with your grocer. I did. You always had to have coupons. Always, always there were the ration coupons.

"We didn't go out much, we sailed our boat, but we didn't go downtown to the movies or theater. We didn't have much company, either.

It's four o'clock in the morning and time to get up and go to work! Lawrence Johnson's two-year-old son Larry Joe blows reveille in the Glenn L. Martin Company trailer park. The elder Johnson worked as a riveter in the nearby assembly plant.

Getting the food together was one of the problems. I remember that at one dinner party we went to the hostess served toasted rolls topped with cheese, with sliced hardboiled eggs on top, and a sauce over all of it. I think back on that dish with joy—it was so good.

"Everything seemed so scarce. My husband and I were always worried about how the war was going.

"Then, there were the blackouts. How I hated the blackouts! Who-o-o-o-o-e-e-e—I can still hear those sirens, and then remember that one, two, three—the lights would go out, wherever you were. I will never forget those sirens. Look, the war changed our lives forever.

"You cannot know the worry we went through, most of us had family in the war. There was always this worry. The war was always in our conversation, in our lives. There was no escaping it. Those screaming sirens…Who-o-o-o-e-e-e…and the relief I felt when the siren rang out an all clear.

"I was always worried. Worried about the soldiers, worried how the war was going, worried about the lines. Always the lines. For food. For gas…

"Do I still think about the war at my age? Yes. We all had shutters, and I remember when the siren sounded we rushed to close the shutters.

"I don't have to close the shutters any more."

Members of the Red Cross Canteen Corps serve lunch at the Blood Donor Service on South Calvert Street, a scene duplicated countless times during the war. After suitable training, the Canteen Corps could do mass feedings in an emergency and operate canteens wherever the Red Cross needed them.

There's a war on, and we just can't get and train waitresses anymore

By the fall of 1942, the sporting fraternity in Baltimore—that feisty collection of politicos, promoters, fighters, card sharks, numbers writers, and horseplayers—had survived many a threat to its existence. But one trauma from which it would never entirely recover was Carl Horn's decision to close down the all-night service in his restaurant, Horn and Horn (on East Baltimore, between Guilford and Holliday, in the Block area), between 1:00 a.m. and 7:00 a.m.

Until that historic decision, Horn's was the one place where the b'hoys could gather all night long to replay yesterday's contests and dope out the oncoming day's events. The gentry would assemble about midnight and talk on toward dawn. In the 1920s the characters were mostly from the sports world; in the 1930s and 1940s they were joined by "guys and dolls" from the nightclubs along the Block and by the politicos from nearby City Hall. Sometimes so many were trying to get in at two and four and five o'clock in the morning that there were lines at the door. But on September 1, 1942, Mr. Horn made an announcement that would send hundreds into the night, homeless. "Times are changing," he said. "There's a war on, and we just can't get and train waitresses anymore, especially ones who will work these morning hours. We will no longer be open all night long."

So early on that morning Mr. Horn put a sign in the window. "Closed, 1 a.m. to 7 a.m." and shooed a procession of mourners out onto the sidewalk. They stood out on the curb, reflectively chewing toothpicks and cigars. "Well," a slickly tailored sporting celebrity was heard to observe philosophically to his companion, "It's the war."

Flitt's war

A fixture in the war years in Baltimore was Ronald Flitt's newsstand at Howard and Fayette streets. He said, "I can get you all of the gasoline stamps you want. The government only sends each car owner the stamps it had allotted him, each stamp good for one gallon at 30 cents a gallon, but I could sell you all the stamps you wanted at 50 cents a gallon." But where did Flitt get all the stamps he sold? And who bought them? Flitt smiled, "Where did I get them? Guys and dolls from the Block—they'd come by and say, 'Here's some stamps, move 'em. Who bought them? Everybody. Lawyers. Bankers. The town's leading citizens. I kept those stamps in a box, in back of the newsstand. Behind the magazines and the newspapers."

But stamps are not all that Mr. Flitt had in the back of his news-

A few of the thousands of workers at the Bethlehem-Fairfield shipyards who looked on as three Liberty ships were launched as part of Labor Day festivities in early September 1942.

stand. The collection included cigarettes, nylon hose, tickets to Ford's, bottles of hard-to-come-by whiskey. "Whiskey was not rationed, but it was murder to find a bottle of your favorite. I'd hold the stuff until somebody would ask me if I knew where they could buy this or that. Whatever they were looking for. One time, a doll from the Block comes by and drops off all of these meat stamps. Sure enough a lady from Roland Park comes by and says, 'Mr. Flitt, I'm giving a party, can you find me some meat stamps?' I told her, 'Well, now. It just so happens that I have this batch of meat stamps.' And that's the way it would go, all during the war. I was open twenty-four hours a day, and I had action all twenty-four of those hours—especially after midnight, when the clubs shut down. There were always plenty of stamps, for whatever you wanted."

Right, Demonstrating the feminine touch as the scrap-metal drive picks up momentum in late September 1942.

Bottom, Scrapping for victory! Residents of the 1000 block East Lombard Street searched their homes from attic to basement for scrap metal and rubber, responding to the military's need, and set the whole mess out on the sidewalk on Sunday, September 20, 1942, for pickup later in the day.

This block was on "Corned Beef Row" in East Baltimore, the heart of the East European Jewish community, and was lined with kosher butchers (see "Brotman's Kosher Meats" *in the background, left*), delis like Attman's, and bakeries like Wartzman's. For sale, too—live chickens from Yankeloff.

Critical to war production, scrap metal and rubber went into guns, planes, ships, tanks, communications apparatus, and things too numerous to list. Uncle Sam considered women's nylon stockings "essential" to the manufacture of parachutes and certain pieces of military gear. American citizens, predictably, made the donating of scrap from one's own personal belongings an act of patriotism. Donating your scrap was your way of winning the war.

Thus, in September 1942, people in Baltimore City and the twenty-three counties of Maryland joined the scrap crusade, searching their homes and gathering up all the metal and rubber scrap they could find, placing it at collection points.

Volunteer truck drivers and loaders, working side by side with soldiers from nearby army bases, made the rounds and collected the scrap: bed springs, baby carriages, boilers, bicycles, waste cans, toys, kitchen utensils, tables and chairs, radiators, garden tools, and any items containing rubber, tin, aluminum, lead, copper, or brass.

In northwest Baltimore, young boys ranging in age from five to fourteen called themselves Junior Commandos and staged local raids in service of scrap collection. Wearing arm bands and carrying American flags and marching to the noise of their own drum corps, they charged into the houses—up into the attics, down into the cellars, out to the garages.

Fifteen-year-old Billy Kolodner and fourteen-year-old Gerald "Colonel" Esterson led the thirty commandos. They told the *Sun* on October 21 that their mission was to "tear the neighborhood apart in search of 250 tons of scrap." The commandos had an official adviser in William Hament, of 2912 Ulman Avenue. Mrs. Emma Engler, of 5203 Cuthbert Avenue, designed the commandos' red and blue arm bands, which read "Bill's Commando Squad."

After collection in the neighborhood, scrap metal went off to one
of six dumps around the city, where
junk dealers arranged to remove it to
their own yards. This one, Cambridge
Iron and Metal, graced a corner of
O'Donnell and Haven. Other firms:
United Iron and Metal, at Lafayette
and Pennsylvania Avenue; Hanover
Iron and Metal, at Charles and McCo-
mas; Edward L. Kelch, at Loch Raven
Road and Fillmore; and B&L Coal, at
Gwynns Falls Parkway and Dukeland.

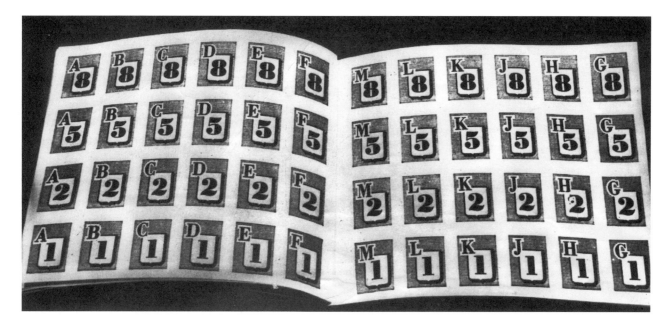

Top, The inside pages of the government's new all-purpose ration book, designated war ration book no. 2, contained coupons that bore both a number and letter. The ration book, announced October 25, 1942, contained eight pages of twenty-four coupons each. Half the pages were colored red; half the pages, green.

Right, Plane spotters at the spotting station situated on the Five Farms Golf Course in Baltimore County, October 29, 1942. Spotters at work are, *left to right,* Mrs. C. G. Morgan and Mrs. A. W. Milch.

My only injury was a bruised knee

In late October, Seaman First Class John M. Chappel, United States Coast Guard, a twenty-year-old African American, came home to 1415 East Preston Street on leave. He had been away ten months, and his story appeared in the *Afro-American* on the thirty-first. He had been in Singapore in January, when his ship was bombed: "One incendiary bomb dropped into a hatch of the ship and killed twenty-five men while I was a short distance away in another hatch. A few months later the ship was torpedoed off the British coast."

Seaman Chappel belonged to the gun crew that retaliated by firing at the enemy sub. "A shell struck it, and turned it over in the water."

In later duty, Chappel was on the USS *Wakefield* when it caught fire, forcing the ship's officers and crew to abandon her. "The fire broke out in the engine room and an explosion followed before the crew could flood the holds. Fortunately, the ship was in a convoy, and all aboard were removed to another ship—after fighting the fire for some fourteen hours. My only injury was a bruised knee, when I bumped against the side of the ship in leaving."

A former Dunbar High School pupil, he had enlisted in the Coast Guard some two years earlier as a mess attendant, and he became a Seaman First Class. He said that he had sailed to almost every major port on the globe.

Opposite, "Before" and "after" on Friday, November 6, 1942. Pictured is the ordinarily frantic, busy, and noisy intersection of Lexington and Park, looking west. On the *left* (southwest corner) stands Julius Gutman's department store; visible in the next block, the May Company department store. On the *right* (the north side of Lexington) is the New Theater, featuring Sonja Henie in the movie *Iceland.* There is no hint in the bustle on display here in downtown Baltimore of what was going to happen next: air-raid alert! Suddenly the air was shattered by the screaming sound of sirens going off, warning everyone within hearing distance that an enemy air raid was imminent. Air-raid wardens leaped up from their desks, grabbed their helmets and arm bands, and went out to protect the civilian population from German bombers! Downtown streets emptied of pedestrians within minutes. Streetcars stopped dead on their tracks, automobiles pulled to the curb, and pedestrians rushed to the nearest air-raid shelters.

The battle of Baltimore and Light

Most streetcars had to run through downtown Baltimore to get to their final destination, turning all of downtown into one vast, bustling, noisy, brightly lit interchange, where war workers—three shifts of them working seven days a week around the clock at plants along Key Highway, in Sparrows Point and Curtis Bay—came in on streetcars from all directions to board at least one other streetcar, sometimes two or three, to get to and from their jobs or home. The churn of war turned small-town, downtown Baltimore into big-time, boomtown Baltimore. Men and women in uniform joined war workers hell-bent on their own wartime destinations. Streetcars clanged and rumbled through clogged streets. Nos. 2, 8, and 26 ran on Fayette; nos. 4, 9, and 14 crossed at Charles and Lexington. Many people found themselves swarming the Baltimore and Light street transfer points.

Eighteen years old in 1942, Jean Rubin (later Levitas), illustrated the typically long commutes. She worked at Eastern Aircraft on Broening Highway. "I was living on Oakley Avenue, off of Park Heights near Pimlico," she recalled for the *Sun* on June 6, 2008. "To get to and from work I took three streetcars, the No. 5 to downtown, and another in Highlandtown, and still another on Broening Highway. We worked one of three shifts, eight in the morning to four in the afternoon, four to midnight, midnight to eight in the morning. It took a long and hard hour and a half each way, often in bad weather, too. I didn't think anything of it."

Mrs. Charles Peace, granddaughter of pharmacist John B. Thomas, who, with his pharmacy school friend and classmate Albert E. Thompson, founded Thomas and Thompson in 1872 at the corner of Baltimore and Light streets, was a young mother in her twenties during the war. "Days and nights, Sundays and holidays, throughout the war," she remembered, "workers—men and some women, all in work clothes and carrying lunch pails—swarmed into the intersecting streets at East Baltimore and Light from all directions. The crossroads was a transfer center; there were streetcar stops at the southeast, the southwest, and the northeast corners, but not the northwest corner— no streetcars ran north on St. Paul Street. Workers were constantly boarding and disembarking, especially when the shifts were changing. They elbowed their way through the crowds to the southeast corner to pay a visit to Thomas and Thompson's drugstore. We were a dependable and familiar way station along their everyday journey. The store was open almost twenty-four hours a day—I think we closed well after midnight and opened again at 5:30 or so. Our big fountain seller was the 'short chocolate,' a glass filled with seltzer, milk, and a shot of chocolate with a handful of graham crackers, free for the taking from a large bowl we kept on the counter. We always kept the bowl full. Some would do their shopping—for such items as raw cotton, aspirin, Mercurochrome, cough syrup.

"The workers, stopping in the store while transferring from one car line to another seemed to look forward to this little break. In Thomas and Thompson's they could enjoy a few moments of escape from their work and from the war news."

Into the bustle of war-plant workers changing streetcars were more than three thousand white-collar workers—going to and coming from the Baltimore Trust Company building on the southwest corner of Baltimore and Light streets. The thirty-four-story structure housed the War Production Board (WPB), Office of Price Administration (OPA), Office of War Information (OWI), Federal Works Authority (FWA), Office of Emergency Management (OEM), War Manpower Commission (WMPC), Federal Power Commission (FPC), Army Officer Procurement (AOP), Internal Revenue Dept. (IRD), Army Specialist Corps (ASC), Securities and Exchange Commission (SEC), Works Projects Administration (WPA), and Office of Civilian Defense (OCD).

Baltimoreans came to refer to the building and its corner as "Little Washington." Men in suits arriving at Penn Station would tell the cab driver "Little Washington" and get straight there.

I don't know of one who has been fired

Nineteen-year-old Edwina Bonnell grew up in Roland Park, graduated from the Bryn Mawr School, came out as a debutante in the Bachelors Cotillion, and (as did many in her glittering social world) decided to forego college and enter war work. In Miss Bonnell's case, it was at Bendix in Towson, a major war contractor.

"This is the first job I ever had," she told the *Sun* on the first of October, 1942. "A lot of my friends, many debutantes, are working in defense plants, and some are working the night shift, too. So far, I am on the day shift. I get up at 7. I've never been late."

Mrs. Charles Markell, secretary of the Junior League, agreed with Lucy Aldrich, daughter of banker Winthrop W. Aldrich, who in New York announced "the end of the debutante" for the duration. She told the *Sun,* "Coming-out parties are dwindling because there are fewer and fewer young men of appropriate age available. I think a lot of the girls would find time for the parties, even with their jobs, if only they could get an interesting and eligible set of males together. The army and navy have ended that possibility." Mrs. Markell added, "The debutantes are working not only at the Bendix plant, where Miss Bonnell is working, but at Glenn L. Martin Company, Bartlett-Hayward Division of the Koppers Company, in local petroleum company laboratories, and in a wide variety of business offices.

"They're making out well; I don't know of one who has been fired. And I do know of a number who have won promotions and raises. Believe me, the girls are much more proud now of a raise than they used to be of popularity at a dance."

Miss Bonnell had it right about her friends working in defense plants and losing interest in the society world of the debutante. There was general consensus among the group that the girls' war jobs left no time for dances and that the armed services were taking more and more of the men. Coming-out parties were going out of fashion, a casualty of war.

Thanksgiving on the home front, 1942

In early November, worried Baltimoreans got good news: the Americans and the British had invaded North Africa, landing between Algiers and Casablanca. It was this country's first full-scale offensive of the war, and some observers at the time were calling it the largest amphibious invasion force ever assembled. In Baltimore, a surprise night air raid was being held. Civilian Defense officials called results "spotty."

On the other side of the world, in the seas off of Guadalcanal, while Baltimoreans were making plans for their Thanksgiving holiday, the light cruiser USS *Juneau* was struck by a torpedo and severely damaged. She was limping to a homeport for repairs when she was struck by two more torpedoes and broke in two. She sank in twenty seconds, with heavy loss of life.

On Thanksgiving Day, war or no war, at St. James's Episcopal Church in the Worthington Valley, fox hunters and hounds gathered for a blessing from the rector; while downtown, kids of every age gathered curbside to watch Hochschild, Kohn's Toy Town Parade; that night, concert lovers crowded the Lyric on Mount Royal Avenue to listen to an all-Russian program featuring Tchaikovsky's Sixth Sym-

Marguerite Walter takes aim, maneuvering the controls of an antiaircraft gun on display at Baltimore and Charles on Pearl Harbor Day—Monday, December 7, 1942. That month Baltimore women turned in eighty thousand pairs (twenty-five thousand pounds) of worn-out silk and rayon hose, salvaging the precious material for use in the manufacture of war-related fabric; homeowners got their fuel-oil allotments; three nightclubs on the Block (2 o'Clock, Gayety, Stardust) were ordered to show cause why their liquor licenses should not be suspended for violations of safety regulations; and on a racquet court on the campus of the University of Chicago, in strictest secrecy, an Italian émigré, the scientist Enrico Fermi, began an experiment that would produce the plan for the first self-sustaining nuclear chain reaction, setting in motion the creation of the first atomic bomb.

Earnest gentlemen, many dressed in
coats and ties, turn in surplus rubber
tires near Franklin and Davis streets,
December 1942.

phony as played by the Baltimore Symphony Orchestra. That same day in the South Pacific saw the Japanese in renewed efforts to reinforce Guadalcanal.

In late November, Baltimoreans learned that Capt. Stuart F. Janney Jr. and Maj. John E. Semmes Jr., both of Baltimore, had fought in the bloody capture of Tarawa in the central Pacific and had come through unscathed.

Casualty of war

On the day after Christmas, a Saturday, in Horn and Horn's restaurant at 123 East Baltimore Street, a rumor was moving along the long, front-to-back counter: at the end of the next day the Charles Street bus (the famous "A") would be discontinued. The news was made harder to bear because on Christmas Eve the last of the storied Charles Street "A" line double-deckers had been taken off the run. The buses, the announcements explained, burned too much gas for a country on wartime footing. What the diners confronted was the harsh news that for the first time within anyone's memory there would be no buses running on Charles Street, from downtown to University Parkway—single-deckers or double—and that alternate streetcar routes had to be considered. "War," some among the disparate crew undoubtedly sighed, "is hell."

At the end of 1942, lines were forming at public and parochial schools for war ration book no. 1, for coffee, sugar, and shoes. No. 2 was for canned vegetables and prepared vegetables and fruits. A registrant had to present "a consumer declaration form" clipped from a newspaper and filled out, telling how many cans the applicant already had on hand. This inconvenience about ration books came in the last days of the year, as Americans on Guadalcanal were engaged in a fierce struggle with the Japanese, and as Baltimoreans were ringing out the old year in Green Spring Valley gatherings and in Highlandtown taverns, and losing themselves, day by day, in their own private routines through a war that held no promise of ending.

Lining up for gas, having your ration card punched, turning in stamps—that was a way of life with gas rationing in effect. Motorists sat in long lines and endless traffic jams. Rumors were continually spreading that new shipments to the gas stations were expected in a day or so. Those "new shipments" seldom arrived when expected. Those who rode the streetcars to work in the hope that when they got home there would be gas available to fill their tanks were usually disappointed.

There was talk of insider favoritism. Many who experienced the gasoline shortage firsthand complained that gas station operators tended to serve only regular customers. These owners, they said, would simply not punch their regular customers' ration cards or would punch over units that had already been perforated.

Others recalled that members of the country clubs who had formerly driven their cars to their clubs were using streetcars and buses during the week and saving their gasoline for weekends.

★ ★ ★ SACRIFICE

Life in Baltimore was defined by shortages—of meat and potatoes and shoes and gasoline—and by the arcane methods and seeming inequities of the system. Some felt constrained by the regulations; others seemed to find ways around them. It was possible but difficult to be distanced from the war. Even if you chose to remain isolated at home and to avoid the crowds downtown, a telegram could find you and give you dreaded news and change your life forever. Whatever you did, wherever and however you lived, the war found you. People flocked to movies and bowling alleys and wrestling and boxing matches, but sooner or later they had to step outside, into the night, and into a world of scarcities and bad news and the unknowable.

They did it in biblical days, and poor people in Europe still do it

As the war lengthened, women's dresses got shorter, and lipstick, rouge, and face powder came in fewer shades.

In this season of Baltimoreans' discontent, conversation was dominated by talk of food shortages, blackouts, bomb drills, shelters, rationing, scrap collections, air-raid drills and air-raid wardens, war bonds, savings stamps, benefit shows, filter centers. The word was out that razor blades were becoming scarce. So, too, tires and gas.

Hy Pusin recalled, "Gas was a serious problem. The Martin management arranged for me to have the gas I needed to drive the fourteen miles back and forth to work, but I was not allowed to use this gas to go downtown or for recreation—to go to the movies or a ball game. To get to those, we took streetcars. They worked quite well. My tires were pretty worn, and nobody could get new ones. There was

Sugar hoarders be warned! Mrs. William Stophlet and her son view a sign appearing in the window of a South Baltimore grocery store warning against the hoarding of sugar.

a terrible shortage of rubber. So shops sprang up offering to 'retread' your tires. Retreading worked. But if you got up around fifty-five miles an hour, the retread would spin off."

Mildred Keiser Strutt remembers that because of the gas shortage she could not get her driver's license until she was twenty-one. "We only had the one car, and my father used it in his work. There was never time, or gas, left over for me to learn to drive."

Baltimoreans responded to shortages in varying ways. Pharmacist W. Harry Smith, whose pharmacy, W. Harry Smith and Son, stood at Edmondson Avenue and Wildwood Parkway, created a novel rationing program of his own, to better serve his long-time customers in the neighborhood. Jerry Kelly, then ten years old and living on the corner of Lyndhurst Street and Cranston Avenue, recalled "Doc's" plan: "Doc Smith printed and distributed to his customers his very own ration cards, good for Hershey bars, Wrigley's chewing gum, and tobacco products—which were sometimes scarce.

"On the days that shipments of candy, gum, and tobacco were delivered to Doc's pharmacy—Tuesday, candy; Thursday, tobacco—I

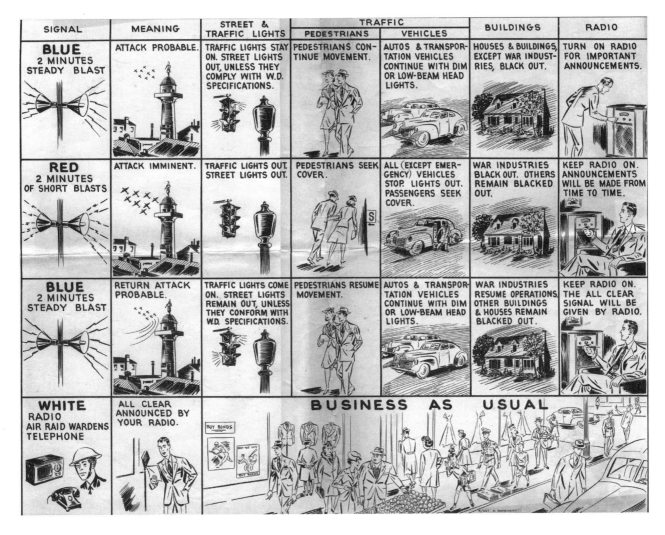

SIGNAL	MEANING	STREET & TRAFFIC LIGHTS	TRAFFIC		BUILDINGS	RADIO
			PEDESTRIANS	VEHICLES		
BLUE 2 MINUTES STEADY BLAST	ATTACK PROBABLE.	TRAFFIC LIGHTS STAY ON. STREET LIGHTS OUT, UNLESS THEY COMPLY WITH W.D. SPECIFICATIONS.	PEDESTRIANS CONTINUE MOVEMENT.	AUTOS & TRANSPORTATION VEHICLES CONTINUE WITH DIM OR LOW-BEAM HEAD LIGHTS.	HOUSES & BUILDINGS, EXCEPT WAR INDUSTRIES, BLACK OUT.	TURN ON RADIO FOR IMPORTANT ANNOUNCEMENTS.
RED 2 MINUTES OF SHORT BLASTS	ATTACK IMMINENT.	TRAFFIC LIGHTS OUT. STREET LIGHTS OUT.	PEDESTRIANS SEEK COVER.	ALL (EXCEPT EMERGENCY) VEHICLES STOP. LIGHTS OUT. PASSENGERS SEEK COVER.	WAR INDUSTRIES BLACK OUT. OTHERS REMAIN BLACKED OUT.	KEEP RADIO ON. ANNOUNCEMENTS WILL BE MADE FROM TIME TO TIME.
BLUE 2 MINUTES STEADY BLAST	RETURN ATTACK PROBABLE.	TRAFFIC LIGHTS COME ON. STREET LIGHTS REMAIN OUT, UNLESS THEY CONFORM WITH W.D. SPECIFICATIONS.	PEDESTRIANS RESUME MOVEMENT.	AUTOS & TRANSPORTATION VEHICLES CONTINUE WITH DIM OR LOW-BEAM HEAD LIGHTS.	WAR INDUSTRIES RESUME OPERATIONS. OTHER BUILDINGS & HOUSES REMAIN BLACKED OUT.	KEEP RADIO ON. THE ALL CLEAR SIGNAL WILL BE GIVEN BY RADIO.
WHITE RADIO AIR RAID WARDENS TELEPHONE	ALL CLEAR ANNOUNCED BY YOUR RADIO.	BUSINESS AS USUAL				

Air-raid signals prepared by the Third Service Command headquarters. This chart, issued February 15, 1943, describes in progressive form the new air-raid warning signals for Baltimore, which were to go into effect the following Wednesday.

would collect the ration cards from customers in the neighborhood. I'd walk over to Doc's, present all the cards, and take delivery for the candy, gum, and tobacco due on each card. Then, I'd make deliveries. I charged a nickel a trip. On a good week I made as much as a $1.25."

People doubled up in their driving commutes, and many were taking the streetcar. Young Bob Rappaport, a student at Park School, found that he could no longer depend on the family chauffeur to take him back and forth from school—gas was too precious. So to get to Park School on Liberty Heights Avenue and Druid Park Drive he walked from his home in Ruxton to the Riderwood Station and took the Pennsylvania Railroad's Parkton local to the Mt. Washington Station in Baltimore City, transferred to the No. 25 to Belvedere Avenue,

Red Cross uniforms mingle with khaki after one of the many scrap drives in wartime Baltimore.

transferred to the No. 31 to Liberty Heights, and then transferred to the No. 32 to Park School. "School started at nine," he said, "I left the house at eight. I was never late."

Shortages in women's hosiery created a war within a war. Scarcities of silk, cotton, nylon, and rayon, and of stockings with seams and stockings without seams, left women scrambling for a place in line in any store that had hose for sale. Stores were fighting suppliers; suppliers were fighting manufacturers. At long last a kind of peace came, and it was the cosmetic companies that came up with a solution (literally) to the problem—a tan fluid that could be painted on legs like face makeup. As for the "seam," women resorted to drawing a black line with a crayon over the brown makeup, from ankle to well above the knee. Or go "seamless."

Many women, weary of the struggle to buy hose, wary of the ag-

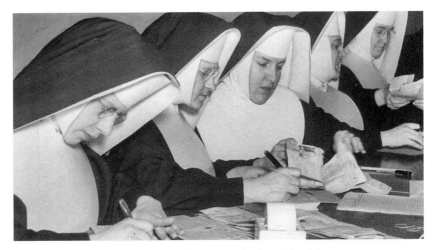

Public and parochial school staffs join in on the job of issuing war ration book no. 2 to consumers on February 23, 1943. *Left to right:* Sisters Mary Timothy, Mary Annette, Mary Roberta, Mary Ancille, and Mary Vinantia, all nuns at St. Casimir's.

ony of painting their legs, and positively fearful of drawing a seam up a leg, went barelegged. The community proved to be accepting. No less a figure than the tenth bishop of Baltimore, Archbishop Michael J. Curley, put his blessing on bare legs in church. "They did it in biblical days," Curley told the *Sun* in July of '42, "and poor people in Europe still do it." Bare legs did not trespass on modesty.

People saved paper clips, toothpaste tubes, bacon grease, chewing gum foil, and rubber bands. Men's suits came without cuffs, patch pockets, or pleats. No new electric refrigerators were being manufactured; if yours died, you did without.

The Department of the Army produced and sent to numerous civilian and military organizations a six-by-nine-inch white card, with red, blue, and black ink, extracting from a speech Gen. George C. Marshall had given at West Point the preceding May to the graduating class of '42, now titled "A Resolution for the New Year" of 1943. "We are determined," read the card, "that before the sun sets on this terrible struggle our flag will be recognized throughout the world as a symbol of freedom on the one hand and of overwhelming power on the other."

Over there, a tough war; over here, pretty good business

As American forces engaged in prolonged and costly battles in Europe, North Africa, and the Pacific, a retailer told a reporter from the *Sun* on February 15 that his business was 500 percent ahead over the same month the year before, and that he was enjoying his best week in the twenty-year history of his store.

Other retailers commented that Baltimoreans were off on a buying

February 23, 1943: This line formed outside a rationing-issue office at Charles and Lombard to get the ration book of the month, ration book no. 2. Thousands who hadn't gotten ration book no. 1, for coffee, sugar and shoes, had an extra line to stand in. No. 2 was for canned and preserved vegetables and fruit. A registrant had to present a "Consumer Declaration Form," clipped from a newspaper and filled out, telling the grocer how many cans were on his or her pantry shelf.

The midnight deadline for sale of canned and preserved foods on the ration list found most Baltimore stores with shelves bare of the items, following a day-long, last-minute buying spree by housewives.

In these same last days of February, heavy fighting was raging in every theater of war. In North Africa the Allies were struggling at the Kasserine Pass; in the Pacific, American submarines were venturing into the dangerous seas approaching Japan. In Baltimore the Retail Merchants Association reported that clothing sales for 1943 were up 47 percent over last year.

Rolling propaganda!

The Victory Garden of Assistant State's Attorney Thomas Biddison, North Charles Street and Melrose Avenue, March 1, 1943. Pictured with Mr. and Mrs. Biddison are, *left to right,* children Robin, Thomas Jr., and Allan. By the spring of 1943, under the guidance of the Baltimore Civilian Mobilization Committee, back yards and vacant lots had been transformed into miniature farms, popularly known as "Victory Gardens."

There were good-size gardens behind the good-size homes in Guilford and Homeland, and small-size back yard gardens behind small-size homes in Highlandtown and Hamilton and Hampden. It was the dream of the committee that the shortage of vegetables in the local grocery store would be made up by the generous harvests from the local soil. In the spring of 1943 there were, by most estimates, twenty thousand Victory Gardens in Baltimore City, yielding corn, peas, carrots, tomatoes, beans, lettuce, broccoli, and who knew what else.

Whole families worked their very own "farm," mostly by day, many by night—using flashlights. Everybody dug in.

binge. One said that expensive watches, diamond rings, and furniture were being bought up—there seemed to be plenty of money around. The customers, merchants said, were not just war workers new to town, with, suddenly, more money than they were used to having, but local residents who were now enjoying greater earning power.

Saturday afternoons were always busy times in downtown Baltimore, the peak of the week's shopping, but on Saturday afternoon, February 27, 1943, the downtown stores were busier than anyone could remember. The counters were being swamped with eager buyers. What was going on was a frenetic response to a rumor that at midnight clothing would be going on the ration list and that each person would be limited to only eighty dollars' worth of clothing a year. Another rumor going around was that women would be limited to one permanent wave a year. Beauty parlors all over town were swamped with requests by women who wanted to have their hair done that same afternoon.

"Clothing stocks are ample," claimed J. W. Mehling, secretary of the Retail Merchants Association, in the *Sun* on February 28. "There is no clothes rationing. Ever since shoe rationing went into effect, clothing sales have been abnormal." A saleswoman summed up the wild afternoon: "People are afraid that they won't be able to buy their outfits, or get their hair done, in time for Easter. I think they are going crazy."

Let's not kid ourselves— while there has been a lessening of discrimination, the prejudice is there

Responding to complaints from African American women who believed they were qualified for many jobs in the war plants but still were not being hired, the director of U.S. Employment Services, Walter Sondheim, admitted in the spring of 1943 that its office was finding it "difficult to place colored women in war jobs." As quoted in the April 17 *Afro-American*, he said that contrary to rumors, his office "was in no way a part of any design to avoid integrating colored women in war industries." He said that, although some employers were specifying in job order requests to his office that only white applicants be sent to them, his agency was doing everything possible to expand job opportunities for colored women. "Let's not kid ourselves. While there has been a lessening of discrimination, the prejudice is there."

The *Afro-American* reported that incidents of prejudice in hiring were coming in daily. It cited the instance of Mrs. Teresa Monroe, of

Baltimoreans lined up by the thousands in Courthouse Plaza (St. Paul, between Lexington and Fayette) on April 22, 1943, to view a captured two-man Japanese submarine. After capturing it at Pearl Harbor, the navy took the submarine apart for study, photographed it, and then sent it on a national tour. If you bought war bonds or stamps, you could take a look inside. During the first hour, visitors bought twenty-four hundred dollars' worth.

2502 Woodbrook Avenue, a vocational school graduate who had been referred to several plants by the employment service and was turned down in each case, and Mrs. Hazel Coats and Mrs. Margaret Ruffine, of 313 North Pine Street, both vocational school graduates in acetylene burning and welding, with 112 hours in a course where a minimum of 80 was required, who were similarly turned down. They were rejected, the *Afro-American* reported, at Maryland Dry Dock, Curtis Bay Coast Guard, and Bethlehem-Fairfield shipyards.

Where were you folks yesterday?

On May 4, 1943, Theodore Roosevelt McKeldin, a Republican, was elected mayor of Baltimore, ousting the four-term Democratic incumbent, Howard W. Jackson. At about the same time, in Tunisia, German troops surrendered unconditionally to American and British forces, bringing an end to the long and hard-fought battle for North Africa. The day after his defeat, Jackson attended a dinner at which he was greeted with loud and prolonged applause. When he took the microphone, he asked, "Where were you folks yesterday?"

If the man has potatoes, let him sell 'em

Potatoes disappeared from stores, and no supplies were received at terminal markets, but on May 24, 1943, the shortage created a wartime drama in East Baltimore. Two housewives spied sacks of potatoes on a truck proceeding along Gough Street on the way to Belair Market.

WARTIME QUESTIONS ANSWERED HERE

"Where can I apply for my gas ration stamps?" "How do I go about car sharing?" "What is the price-controlled cost of a quart of milk?" Life in wartime Baltimore could be confusing, what with shortages and an avalanche of regulations, but local offices of the War Price and Rationing Board offered some help. This one stood on Ayrdale Avenue in May 1943.

Within minutes crowds were storming the truck, and, according to accounts, hundreds of people bought thousands of potatoes in less than an hour, and two lucky truck drivers were five hundred dollars richer.

Details of the near-riot came out in the *Sun* the following day. It seems that Sam Palmisano and his brother, Frank, were driving along with their truckload of potatoes when the two women caught a fleeting glimpse of the fifty sacks of the valuable cargo passing by.

In those days of shortages, one glimpse was enough. In seconds the women ran out into the street and persuaded the Palmisanos to stop the truck, open the sacks, and sell them some of the precious spuds. Word got out and spread, and before the two women could buy ten pounds each at ten cents a pound, the price agreed upon, crowds were milling about the truck.

The plot thickens here as Patrolman Max Oettel, Eastern District, who also had gotten the word, arrived on the scene and promptly arrested the Palmisanos for selling without a license. Dutifully, the Palmisanos, driving a truck with a depleted stock of potatoes, reported to the police station.

The Schoolfield family goes to war! According to a *Sun* report of May 26, 1943, the pilot of a Flying Fortress that had made a score of raids on Germany, Lt. Charles T. Schoolfield, of Baltimore, had named the plane *Sis* for his elder sister, Gertrude, *right*. Their sister Grayce Schoolfield, *below*, had already joined the WAVES. In the article, Gertrude revealed that she was going overseas with the Red Cross.

Baltimore, Wednesday, **THE EVENING SUN** May 26, 1943

Acute Gas Crisis 'Apparently' Is Past: Blakely

Sister Of Air Fighter Is Going Overseas Also

Pickett Tr Men For N Army Unit

LIEUT. C. T. SCHOOLFIELD
Named his Fortress "Sis"

GERTRUDE SCHOOLFIELD
"Sis" is going overseas

GRAYCE SCHOOLFIELD
This "Sis" is a WAVE

After posting seven dollars collateral, Sam left for City Hall to buy a license. Frank stood guard over the truck and its load of potatoes.

Meanwhile, police lieutenant John Kenealy, fearing a black market was about to start in front of the station house, telephoned OPA officials. The reply was: "If the man has potatoes, let him sell 'em."

The Palmisanos did, the moment Sam got back with the license. Within minutes hundreds of men, women, and children were milling around the truck. Each customer was limited to a ten-pound sack.

Potato merchants Sam and Frank Palmisano later reported to the police station and received a proper hearing in front of Magistrate Samuel Campanaro on the charge of selling without a license. Charges were dismissed.

Those who missed the Great Palmisano Potato Sale had to scrounge about for other starches—hominy, rice, spaghetti, and macaroni.

An Office of War Information photographer found these women arc welders taking time out for lunch and laughs in the pipe shop of Bethlehem Fairfield shipyards, May 1943.

Over here, over there; summer of 1943

On June 23, 1943, Baltimore had a surprise two-hour and twenty-one minute blackout test, which the Eastern Defense Command of the Army Air Force declared "valuable." In the unfamiliar darkness, one man died of injuries suffered when he fell down cellar steps; another man was stabbed to death.

All the while, the zany, anything-goes wrestling matches at the Coliseum on Monroe Street went on—to the delight of wildly cheering crowds. One night the Golden Terror lost to Maurice the Angel; one patron, upset at the way things were going, leapt up into the ring and ripped the shirt from the referee's back. A woman sitting at ringside was ejected from the area when she tossed cups of ice onto the canvas. In another bout, wrestler Milo Steinborn threw Babe Sharkey over the ropes and then knocked referee Ed Brockman down for trying to get Babe back in the ring.

Patrons coming out of the Coliseum those early summer nights would read in the morning paper about Gen. Douglas MacArthur's historic Operation Cartwheel—a series of daring assaults designed to capture the vital city of Rabaul in the Solomon Islands and thus committing American lives to what would be one of the early, hard-fought steps along the road to Tokyo.

The sheer numbers of servicemen who found themselves in Baltimore during the war were nowhere more evident than in Penn Sta-

Where is everybody? This is Charles Street at Lexington on Monday, May 31, 1943, looking north (with the Washington Monument in the distance) at ten o'clock on the Memorial Day holiday. Gasoline rationing was in effect.

The rules governing gas rationing were by this time well known, although reliably complicated and sometimes confusing. Allotments were based on need, as related to work considered essential, and in particular, war work. Class A drivers got the least amount of gas: for pleasure only or for driving less than six miles per day in connection with their work. Class X, Quota X entitled holders to unlimited quantities of gasoline, reserved for ambulances, hearses, taxicabs, doctors and nurses on duty, municipal officials, and construction and repair vehicles rendering public service. The long lines of Sunday drivers disappeared,

and in their stead were long lines at gas stations. The same cars.

That summer (as American soldiers were wading ashore in Sicily) the Baltimore Transit Company made drastic cuts in the city's bus lines to save gasoline: "Affected are the Halethorpe line, halted east of Franklin and Charles Street; the cross town line, which goes only to Falls Road, except on the all-night run and during shift changes at the Woodberry mills." Streetcar service would substitute.

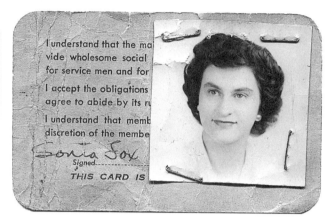

In 1943, twenty-year-old Sonia Fox (later Schnaper) was working as a buyer in the book department of the Hochschild Kohn department store at Howard and Lexington, where, she recalled, the word was going around the office that the USO at 305 West Monument was holding reception/dances for servicemen on Sunday afternoons. "All the guys I knew and would have been going out with," she said, "were away, and the USO dances seemed interesting. So my girlfriend, Dona LaPides [later Colton] and I, on a Sunday afternoon, took the No. 32 streetcar from where we were living on Liberty Heights Avenue, near Mondawmin, to Park Avenue and walked over to the YMHA.

"We knew the chaperone—it was Dona's mother—and so we were invited in to join the group. At around five o'clock, we served the guys supper. We had a jukebox that provided music to dance to. Most all of the soldiers were stationed at Aberdeen and Edgewood and Fort Meade.

"But I never recall any relationships building up among the girls and the guys week to week. Maybe that was because the army bases seemed to be sending different groups of guys each week."

tion, at Charles Street between Mount Royal Avenue and East Lanvale Street. It offered a window onto the war—the tension of arrival and farewell; lovers and loved ones embracing as they wondered when and if they would see each other again; groups of soldiers and sailors jostling through an immovable mass of crowds to board trains for destinations that held uncertain futures. Watching the round-the-clock melee, the management of the railroad, out of patriotism and a well-intentioned but hopeless attempt to relieve the crush, built the Servicemen's Canteen Lounge.

An addition to the station's east wall, the lounge offered a reading room, writing room, lounge, and snack bar. But on Saturday afternoon, July 25, 1943, it offered something else: a wedding.

The young ladies of Hamilton Junior High School did their bit by conducting a campaign for canned goods, presumably to help stock Red Cross or USO kitchens.

The bride and bridegroom, accompanied by the wedding party, were among the early guests in the lounge and canteen, which had opened for the first time that morning.

The bride was Katharine Ann Wiedefeld, daughter of Mr. and Mrs. Henry Wiedefeld, of the 900 block of East Chase Street. The bridegroom was Sgt. Paul Raymond Schultheis, of the 2000 block Kennedy Avenue. The couple was married by the Rev. Thomas B. Zinkand, assistant pastor of St. John's Catholic Church. Then Mr. and Mrs. Schultheis waited to leave on their honeymoon. Soldiers and sailors lounging about the station were invited to kiss the bride. Many did.

In mid-August the word was out that William Ewald's victory garden at 4212 Tuscany Court had grown tomato plants six and seven feet tall. At the time, American forces were fighting their way into Messina, putting the entire island of Sicily under the control of Allied armies.

Italy surrendered September 8, 1943. The news was welcomed all over Baltimore, but with particular vigor in Little Italy. "Thank God!" declared Congressman Thomas "Tommy" D'Alesandro Jr. "I always knew the Italian people had no enmity against the United States." Mama Emma of the Roma restaurant, at 231 High Street in Little Italy, said, "I pray. I do everything. It's great news!" The bars and restaurants on High, Fawn, and Albemarle streets and along the Eastern Avenue section of Little Italy served free drinks.

A Victory Corps class at Baltimore City College takes instruction in signaling and nautical knot tying from James C. Leonhart. In September 1943, the war weighed on the shoulders of high-school boys and girls—in classrooms and on drill fields, in or out of uniform. Wilmer DeHuff, principal of Polytechnic Institute, explained to the *Sun* that Victory Corps members at Poly studied airplane recognition, radio and Morse code, and boat construction. They took courses designed to prepare young men for military service.

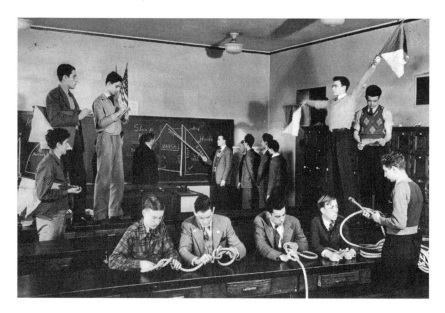

Right, Victory Corpsmen at Baltimore Polytechnic Institute, September 14, 1943. They carried wooden "guns."

Bottom, Students at Western High School on Gwynns Falls Parkway, said principal Mildred Coughlin, would continue their volunteer work for the Red Cross at hospitals and ration boards and in the school's own campaign to sell war bonds and stamps. "The course will serve the students in future wartime jobs," she explained. "Mathematics and science are being emphasized. The girls will wear no uniforms, but will wear Victory Corps arm bands, which will be awarded to those who complete the required corps work."

Top, A wedding being performed by Rabbi Charles A. Rubenstein, formerly of Baltimore's Har Sinai Congregation, at the 305 West Monument Street Y and USO. In the picture, save for the rabbi, all participants in the wedding—bride, groom, best man, bridesmaid—are in the military. The wedding ceremony is being performed under the traditional wedding canopy, or *chuppah.*

Right, In the spring of 1943, officials of war production plants announced that, though all women workers were now wearing slacks, they would soon be wearing their work uniforms and that they would be required to wear hairnets or head coverings and low-heeled shoes as precautions against accidents. Open-toed shoes were not allowed, and neither was "primping into mirrors, and putting on lipstick or powder." This railroad worker probably did not have to be told.

On the evening of October 1, 1943, members of the Maryland State Militia, armed and wearing gas masks, took up their positions on Lexington near Charles, ready for the Germans—should their forces be sighted rolling up Charles Street intent on storming the Century (first floor) and Valencia (second floor) theaters.

The Locust Point Ferry's wartime crap games

For war workers who lived on the east side of the Inner Harbor, in Highlandtown and Canton, and who worked over on Locust Point on the southwest side, the trip to work and back around the harbor by car pool could, in those hectic three-shift days and nights, be harrowing, frustrating, and time-consuming.

There was a better way: instead of driving around the harbor (over to Pratt and Light, south to Key Highway) workers took a ferry across the harbor, from the foot of Broadway (Fells Point) to the foot of Haubert Street in Locust Point, in South Baltimore. The running time was four minutes. But that across-the-harbor ferry ride offered the workers more than just speed. The workers themselves converted the ferryboats into floating casinos.

Once aboard, the men (some women) quickly settled into two compatible groups—card players and crapshooters. An observer noted, "The decks have lost most of their glamour since these workmen have swarmed over them, shooting dice and playing poker." He said it appeared the crap games were the same ones, continued day to day by the same players. He said that there were reports of workmen borrowing dimes to get home, after the "bones" had gone against them.

One of the favorite places for crapshooting was the roof of the pilothouse. On one occasion a visitor, in a compartment directly below the pilothouse, heard a "pattering" up there and looked quizzically at his host. "That," the host explained, "ain't birds dancin'. Them boys up there is shootin' crap."

He said it was that way all the way over and all the way back, through four years of three-shift days and nights.

We could drive anywhere, but we couldn't live anywhere

"In those days, we called ourselves Negroes," recalled Frances Lockwood. "We didn't call ourselves 'blacks' until much later. During the war we were living quite comfortably in the neighborhoods above North Avenue on and around Druid Hill Avenue, Madison Avenue, Division Street. They called the area the 'Gold Coast' or 'Striver's Row.' It was said in the Negro community that if you had lived above North Avenue you had made it! They were neighborhoods of homeowners and family households. The men and women held very good jobs as butlers and maids in the homes of the very rich white families.

"We lived at 2346 McCulloh Street, because my daddy had a very good job—he was captain in the dining room of the Belvedere Hotel. If he'd been white he'd have been a maitre d'. Our neighbors were among Baltimore's prominent Negro families.

"I was twenty-two years old, and a school teacher, on that December morning when I heard that war had broken out. You see, Negroes in Baltimore did not have all of those public places to go that white people had, and so a favorite thing to do on Sunday mornings was to take a Sunday drive. And I was out for a Sunday drive that morning with a young man I was dating at the time, George Gibson. When we heard the news on the car radio, we immediately turned around and we each went home. We were shocked.

"But I continued teaching—the first grade at an elementary school on Caroline Street and I was, of course, living at home. Then I met William V. Lockwood, a fine and very promising young man who was a high school teacher and living on Myrtle Avenue, and we became romantically involved. In the summer of 1942, he was drafted and became one of the first Negroes in the country to be admitted into Officer's Candidate School. In a few months he would be 'Lieutenant Lockwood' in the Army Corps of Engineers in Fort Belvoir in Virginia. He was transferred to a base in Missouri and I went there to visit him, and we got married there near his base on September 1, 1942. I came home, and I found myself pregnant.

"In December of 1943, I went to Louisiana to see him off for overseas duty. In a few weeks I heard from him—he was in England.

"I took up life in wartime in a very segregated Baltimore. We could drive anywhere, but we couldn't *live* anywhere!

"I remember well the air-raid warnings, and the wardens patrolling the neighborhoods, making sure your lights were out during the drill. But most of all, I missed a washing machine. Mine broke down, and I had a new baby, and I had to wash all my baby's clothes on a washboard. I tried every way to get a washing machine but couldn't get one. Very few Negroes had a car during the war, so gas rationing to us was not a problem.

"But even if there were washing machines available in those days of scarcities, Negroes didn't stand much of a chance of getting one. The only stores where we could buy anything were Brager-Eisenberg, Julius Gutman, and those along Pennsylvania Avenue. It was so bad for us in Baltimore during those wartime days that we used to go to Philadelphia to shop for what we needed. None of the better stores—Hutzler's, Hochschild's, Stewart's—would serve us. If you walked into Stewart's you had to have a note 'from your Madame' saying that you were 'her servant, shopping for her.' If you didn't have the note you couldn't enter the store. If somehow you did get in, you were asked to leave.

"My boyfriend, who became my husband, went into the army as a private and came out of a segregated army as a major, and that accomplishment astonished people—black and white. Before he went into the army he wanted to go to the University of Maryland School of Engineering, but he was told, 'You are a Negro. You cannot get into a school of engineering; be a teacher or a social worker.' So he ended up in education. As late as the war years, if you applied to the University of Maryland they would pay your tuition to whatever college you could get into—anywhere in the country as long as it wasn't the University of Maryland.

"I never will forget the time I was traveling on a bus going to see my husband in Virginia, for a ceremony at which he was to be commissioned a second lieutenant, just before he was to be sent overseas.

I boarded in Baltimore and was seated in the middle of the bus. When we got to Virginia, the bus stopped and a policeman came back to where I was sitting and said I had to get to the back of the bus. I was furious. I said, 'Listen! I am going to see my husband, who is a soldier in this war. He is going to be commissioned as a second lieutenant in the service of this country! And he is going overseas tomorrow.' And he said, 'Lady, if you don't get to the back of this bus, war or no war, I am going to lock you up.'

"I got up and moved. What was I to do?"

Home for Christmas, via the *Sun* and radio

On December 8, 1941, a full-page ad appeared in the *Baltimore News-Post,* under the caption "WBAL Radio News." The "news" the station was sending out was the result of a nationwide survey that, WBAL claimed, showed NBC to be "the network most people listen to most." NBC in Baltimore was WBAL radio.

The ad went on to list the fourteen most popular half-hour radio programs—all on WBAL radio. Included were Edgar Bergen and Charley McCarthy, Fibber McGee and Molly, Eddie Cantor, Burns and Allen. A second message of the ad, not as clear, was that national radio networks dominated the airwaves. Whatever air time the network didn't use, the local station filled with local talent: Fred Robbins, Carroll Warrington and His All-Girl Chorus, Uncle Jack's and Uncle George's Kiddies Clubs, Hi Jinks with Bob Iula's orchestra, Brent Gunts, Phil Christ, Henry Hickman, Walter Linthicum, Don Spatz, Lew Corbin, Richard Dix, Flo Ayres, Murray Slatkin.

But for listener interest, few broadcasts in Baltimore during the war, locally or nationally, could compare with the broadcast at 12:45 p.m. over WFBR, Baltimore (1300 on the dial, located at Charles Street and North Avenue) on Christmas Day, 1943. The hour-long broadcast was billed by its sponsor, the *Sun,* as a "Christmas Broadcast to Bring the Voices of Soldiers Home"—which it surely did.

The broadcast originated, the *Sun* reported, "from an Army camp somewhere in England where invasion forces are training" and from a bomber base of the Eighth Air Force elsewhere in the British Isles, and it was made possible through special arrangement with the Army Special Services and the British Broadcasting Corporation. Here (as the *Sun* reported on December 26) is what was beamed into Baltimore (and eight small towns in Virginia and Pennsylvania) that Sunday noon, and some reactions to the broadcasts by loved ones.

To start the program, listeners heard three of the masters of ceremony: Lt. Col. Ben Lyon, a Maryland actor attached to the Eighth Air Force; Warrant Officer William Fisher from Frederick, Maryland; and Cpl. Jean [*sic*] Lowenthal of Baltimore. Corporal Lowenthal's five-year-old daughter Marianne was listening and dancing around a radio in Ocean View, Delaware, and shouting, "That's my Daddy!" Mrs. Lowenthal said, "I laughed a little, and I cried a little. We haven't seen him in fifteen months."

Sgts. Benny Blubaugh, Jose Casanova, and Sol Lurie of Baltimore then sang "Java Jive." Sergeant Blubaugh's wife was listening, along with in-laws in their home at 510 North Monroe Street. She said, "It was a big thrill to hear him sing, but I had hoped to hear him say a few words."

Corporal Lowenthal introduced a recently married couple—Pvt. Melvin Carbaugh of Frederick, Maryland, and his new English wife, Dorothy. The broadcast gave the bride her first opportunity to tell her new parents-in-law that she was "looking forward to visiting them." Sgt. Melvin Sheer of Baltimore and Cpl. Frank Meneguzzo, from Pringle Hill, near Wilkes-Barre, Pennsylvania, followed with a guitar and violin rendition of "Stardust."

Cpl. Martin Willen of Baltimore sang a song to his wife Miriam, "Just a Little Love, a Little Kiss," and sent along his best wishes to his uncle and aunt, Mr. and Mrs. Solomon Willen, of 3619 Wabash Avenue.

The program was turned over to Lt. Col. Lyon. His mother, Mrs. Ben Lyon, was listening at the home of her daughter, Mrs. Ben Meyers, 7301 Park Heights Avenue. She had last seen her son in California, in July. She said, "I thank the *Sun* for making my Christmas complete."

Lt. William Hickey, whose wife was home at 404 South Smallwood and whose parents were nearby at 223 South Stricker Street, told the audience that he had flown in five missions as a bombardier since his arrival in England. He said, "I'd rather be in Baltimore than over Wilhelmshaven. I remember that on Christmas Eve our whole family used to go to midnight Mass at St. Martin's, a West Baltimore landmark. I went to school there." He said he missed the fried rabbit dinner his mother used to prepare when the family returned from Mass.

Maj. John C. Bishop, a Flying Fortress squadron leader and a veteran of twenty-two missions, was remembering Queenstown, his hometown on Maryland's Eastern Shore, and "the Eastern Sho' Christmas dinner" his wife was having with his parents—"with oysters in the dressing and some of my mother's plum pudding for dessert." His wife, visiting with his mother over Christmas in Queenstown, said, "It was so wonderful to hear my husband. I can't believe all of this has happened."

Sgt. Cody Wolf of Catonsville said that his "Christmas was not too bad." He said, "I've been thinking a lot about Catonsville." His parents and his wife, Emma, and their sixteen-month-old daughter Margaret Ann, were listening. Emma said, "His voice sounded good." She heard the broadcast in Sergeant Wolf's home at 58 Wade Avenue in Catonsville.

Sgt. Joseph Klein, of 1405 Clarkson Street in Baltimore, was a member of the ground crew stationed in England fifteen months, and he was spending his fourth Christmas away from home. He remembered Southern High School and working at Sparrows Point.

Capt. Charles Schoolfield, of 1808 Sulgrave Avenue in Mt. Washington, who had earned a Distinguished Flying Cross with Oak Leaf Cluster and an air medal with three Oak Leaf Clusters, said his squadron led a raid on Schweinfurt, battling enemy fighters for an hour and twenty minutes. Captain Schoolfield said that he was still unmarried but that he corresponded with an army nurse from Baltimore, Edith Doyle, who was stationed at Camp Livingston in Louisiana. His mother, listening with family and friends at the family's Mt. Washington home, said, "It was as if our boy had dropped in to see us."

Lt. Woodrow Wilson Thomas, of 504 Harwood Avenue, used the occasion to tell all his family and friends in Baltimore that he was engaged to Miss Rita Hilliard, of 4144 Eierman Avenue.

Other news that late December (1943) and early January (1944) was less cheerful. In Italy, despite the fierceness of the American attack on the village of Cassino, the Germans were holding. In Baltimore, five hundred employees of the Point Breeze plant of Western Electric went on strike after negotiations over several months and a federally authorized strike vote failed to resolve the problem: union employees wanted the company to provide separate sanitary facilities for "white" and "colored."

The No. 32 streetcar served Wood-lawn, Liberty Heights, Whitelock Street, Linden Avenue, and on to Park Avenue and into downtown, for transfer to any number of routes to work, movies, restaurants.

Champagne and moonshine

On the afternoon of January 6, 1944, in the Bethlehem-Fairfield ship-yards on Key Highway, no less than Mary Pickford ("America's Sweet-heart" of the silent movies) was about to crack a bottle of champagne across the bow of the Liberty Ship SS *Samnid*. Standing behind her to provide musical accompaniment was a threesome known as the O'Dell Brothers.

They were dressed in torn red plaid shirts that had the look of what is called "country." "But we're hillbillies," Orville O'Dell, who played guitar, told an observer. "That's what we are, hillbillies." Add-ed brother George, who played fiddle, "Yeah, we're from the hills." Brother Stanley, who played mandolin, chimed in, "Yep, way back in them hills! All right, boys," he shouted to the brothers, "let her rip."

Children's dresses, sweaters, and layettes made by adult volunteers of the Baltimore Red Cross Chapter and Junior Red Cross members are stacked high at the chapter headquarters at 204 Guilford Avenue, January 21, 1944. They were to be shipped on the SS *Cold Harbor* to Europe. Mary Ann Jacobson, dressed in a very junior Red Cross uniform, holds a doll she will give up for a youngster abroad.

Not long after Pearl Harbor the hiring of women as war workers proved so successful that the word was out— the war plants would hire qualified women just as fast as they applied. Here, on April 10, 1944, Julia Handler, age eighteen and a graduate of Patterson Park High School, works on an assembly line at Glenn L. Martin's.

An official of the company said that they were going to need a lot more help and would be looking to women to make up a large part of that help. He said that a requirement for employment would be vocational training in the applicant's background. He mentioned specifically the large numbers who had been trained at Girls Vocational School and School #250.

Lay that pistol down, babe, lay that pistol down.
Pistol Packing Momma, lay that pistol down.

In those wartime days in Baltimore, Bethlehem-Fairfield was hiring hundreds of workers a week to build cargo ships for duty in the North Atlantic and the South Pacific. But for Baltimore, the story was not where the ships were going but where the shipyard workers were coming from—locales made obvious from the graffiti scrawled on the tool sheds.

Summerfield, West Virginia
Galax, Virginia
Ashland, Kentucky
Sharpsburg, North Carolina

Drinking beer in a cabaret and was I havin' fun,
'Til one night she caught me right and now I'm on the run.

During the war, hundreds of thousands of these workers came down from the hills of Appalachia to the war plants of Baltimore. They not only brought their working skills with them, they brought their music, which quickly found its way onto Baltimore radio stations.

When the war was over, many went home (including, as far as it is known, the O'Dell Brothers), but many stayed—adding their historic culture to historically polyglot Baltimore.

It didn't take long to learn the job, and after you got used to it, it wasn't hard

"I was in my late twenties when I heard that the Maryland Dry Dock, which repaired ships up on dry dock, was hiring women," Sarah Dittinger Chandler remembered. "I was living with my husband and my mother and my two young daughters in the 2100 block of Barclay Street, near Greenmount Avenue, so I went down there. I took the No. 13 on North Avenue and transferred a couple of times. But I got there. It took maybe forty minutes. Plenty of women were applying for jobs at Maryland Dry Dock at the time. I applied for the job and sure enough I got it. I became a helper to a sheet-metal worker.

"What I did, I helped my boss, a guy named Wade. He lived in Hampden. Our job was to bend three- and four-foot lengths of sheet metal around asbestos-covered pipes. Somebody else had wrapped the asbestos. It didn't take me long to learn the job, and after you got used to it, it wasn't hard.

Workers at Bethlehem-Fairfield shipyards construct Victory ships in the spring of 1944.

"My sister Kitty, she worked there, too. We worked the daytime shift. Eight in the morning until four in the afternoon. We got half an hour off for lunch and two fifteen-minute breaks, one in the morning, one in the afternoon. Mostly, during our time-outs we'd take a smoke. My mother watched the two children at home. It was hard, but we survived.

"I worked six, sometimes seven days a week. All the women did. Didn't do much else. Like going to movies and things. Just worked. Wade was easy to work for. He'd inspect everything I did and then he'd say, 'Good girl! Good girl!'

"Sometime before the war was over, I had to quit. My mother could no longer take care of my children. I worked at Maryland Dry Dock about two years.

"What with work and taking care of my children and my husband working and the war and everything, well, yes, it was hard. But we survived. Honey, we survived. Lemme tell you, we survived."

Flower Mart opens, war goes on

On Wednesday, May 10, 1944, the annual Flower Mart opened with its traditional Mardi Gras atmosphere, offering a bright fair of flowers and sunshine and peppermint lemon sticks, all in the spirit of the very hospitable Women's Civic League. But this year the Flower Mart, like every institution in Baltimore at the time, had gone to war. At eleven o'clock that morning, to cheering and marching music, uniformed WACS (Women's Army Corps), navy WAVES (Women Accepted as Volunteers for Emergency Service), SPARS (Women's Coast Guard Auxiliary; the acronym is for "Semper Paratus, Always Ready"), women marines, and Red Cross workers staged a colorful parade around the Washington Monument to start the opening ceremony. Children carrying tiny flags fell in with the marchers; it was Baltimore's civic celebration of itself and of spring—the music and picnicking and gardening in a timely partnership with patriotism on display, brave and colorful in the morning sun. But the celebrants, in such a mood and place, could not appreciate the odd timing of the occasion: in Italy the Allies were engaged in a massive all-out artillery barrage on the town of Cassino, energizing a months-long bloody offensive that had already turned the town to rubble. At the Flower Mart, late in the afternoon in the fading light, patrons sat at small tables, Paris-style, around the monument, enjoying the last few hours of the festival. As the crowds thinned, light refreshments were served, setting a languid mood—while in Washington and London, distanced from the flowers and lemons and peppermint sticks, final touches were being put on the plans for Operation Overlord, the long-awaited and epochal invasion of the continent. D-Day had been set for early June.

Don't you know it's Straw Hat Day in Baltimore?

Year after year, in the months leading up to May 15, the men of Baltimore wore felt hats. In those prewar and war years, a felt fedora hat was part of the uniform of the well-dressed Baltimore male. But during the night of May 14/15 a transformation occurred, and in the morning these same men were wearing, suddenly, straw hats. (A "straw hat" was made of fibers and shaped like a felt hat or was a "flat top," sometimes called a "boater" or a "skimmer.")

The precise date of the change—fedora to straw—was not by chance; it was "mandated" nationally by the men's hat industry, which had created what it called "Straw Hat Day," an undisguised commercial promotion. The occasion had special significance here in Baltimore because the city had become the largest center for the manufacture of straw hats in the world, and Baltimoreans were only too happy to perpetuate the spirit of it all. "The first straw hats to be made in Baltimore," according to the late Lester Levy, whose firm, M. S. Levy and Sons, was founded by his grandfather and was, from 1874 to 1958, the largest straw hat manufacturer in Baltimore, "came from John Q. Taylor in the early 1870s. Mr. Taylor had a unique idea. He brought to Baltimore braids that he had purchased from the Mackinac Indians in northern Michigan and fashioned them into 'straw' hats. The idea took." Soon, other hat manufacturers sprang up in Baltimore—among them Brigham-Hopkins and Townsend-Grace.

"I distinctly remember," Mr. Levy recalled, "being out in the ballpark one May 15. It was during the war. I saw a man wearing a felt hat, and a fan wearing a boater reached across a few seats and snatched it. He shouted at him, 'Don't you know it's Straw Hat Day in Baltimore?'"

MIA

On a night in late May or early June of 1944 (exact date unknown) an American aircraft, having completed its bombing mission in Italy, was flying back to its base when it took flak and burst into fire. The crew prepared to abandon ship and parachute out, one by one, when they discovered that their gunner was suffering from a shrapnel wound in his leg; worse, loss of blood had rendered him unconscious, unable to parachute out on his own. The crew members made a decision: they strapped the wounded gunner into his chute gear and threw him out of the plane; one of them pulled the rip cord on his parachute, opening it and allowing the wounded and unconscious gunner to drop slowly into enemy territory. As the story was reported in the American press, by the time the gunner hit the ground, he had regained consciousness—to understand that German soldiers had seized him, that he was now a prisoner of war in Yugoslavia, and that he would be sent immediately to a prison camp in Germany.

He was Bernard Blum, from Baltimore, the son of Mr. and Mrs. David Blum, of 3116 Tioga Parkway. He was graduated from Baltimore City College in 1942 and later that same year joined the army. In November of 1943 he married Shirley Kirsh, and they lived at 2216 Loyola Southway. Early in 1944, Sergeant Blum went overseas.

In September of 1944 his wife received word that her husband was alive, but a prisoner of war in Germany. Then, for weeks on end, she heard nothing.

It's my duty here to inform you that the Allied forces are, as we are speaking, landing troops in Normandy

On Tuesday, June 6, as the Baltimore Orioles were moving up from fifth place into fourth in the International League, taking the best of Newark and Rochester, General Dwight D. Eisenhower launched one of the greatest military ventures in history with the words, "OK, let's go!"—thus sending Allied forces across the English Channel. Oriole Manager Tommy Thomas said that Oriole players Howie Moss and Abe Tiedeman had passed their induction physicals and would be moving on. They were awaiting the draft call and would probably miss the rest of the season.

Many workers bound for their jobs that morning learned about D-Day from the newsboys on the streets and aboard streetcars shouting, "Extra! Extra!" Other Baltimoreans, snapping on their radios at breakfast time, heard it and quickly aroused others in the family. Many churches, normally closed on weekdays, were opened and prayer services held. Taverns closed.

At lunch hour downtown, people jammed the sidewalks east and north of the *Sun* building at Charles and Baltimore streets to read bulletins flashing across the Trans Lux.

Baltimoreans learned from a dispatch issued by the Chicago *Daily News* Foreign Service that Capt. Leonard T. Schroeder, of Baltimore (North Linthicum), may have been the first American or the first soldier of any Allied nation to go ashore in the June 6, 1944, landing.

Phyllis Kolker Schreter, a senior attending her graduation from Goucher College, was seated in the Lyric Theater that same morning when the news broke in Baltimore. She recalls, "The commencement speaker was the British ambassador to the United States, Lord Halifax. He came to the podium and said, 'It's my duty here to inform you that the Allied forces are, as we are speaking, landing troops in Normandy.' Cheers went up and that was the end of the ceremony. Almost everybody in the hall that day had a brother or a cousin or a friend or a parent in the war and so we all began to share our joy with one another. I think we got our diplomas but there was no going on with the graduation ceremony!"

Hy Pusin and his co-workers at Glenn L. Martin heard the news

Late in the evening of Monday, July 3, 1944, some sixty-five hundred fans seated in old Oriole Park, at Twenty-ninth and Greenmount, watched a heartbreaker: the Baltimore Orioles (International League) blew the game to the Syracuse Chiefs in the tenth inning.

Blue in defeat, the fans filed out of the park, many to board the No. 8 streetcar (Towson to Catonsville) for home, not knowing that, within hours, there would be more for Baltimore baseball fans to mourn than this loss to Syracuse: at about 4:30 the following morning, July 4, a monstrous fire broke out in the park and destroyed it—it would turn out—forever.

Those sixty-five hundred fans had watched the last game ever to be played by the Orioles at their Greenmount Avenue home. The fire burned so quickly that six alarms were turned in within fifteen minutes—bringing

to the scene not only all of those fire engines but also Mayor Theodore R. McKeldin, who, according to eyewitness accounts, was busy handing out autographed pictures of himself.

Oriole Park at Greenmount could hold about twelve thousand seated, fourteen thousand standing, and it had one covered deck running from first base to third base. Bleacher seats (simple, backless benches) took up a small area out in right field. The park was a green-painted wooden clapboard affair that was a firetrap from the day it was built in 1914, and on this night it burned like kindling. Most of Baltimore's available fire engines, with assists from neighbors with garden hoses pouring on water from their next-door rooftops, were powerless to stop the searing flames, which shot several stories high.

By sunrise the park was a pile of

smoking, charred debris. Tommy Thomas, then manager of the club, announced that the July Fourth game (a sellout) couldn't be played anywhere because all the team's equipment had been lost in the fire, but that the season would be resumed in Municipal Stadium when and if new equipment could be obtained. All the fans and most of the players were dismayed at the news, save one—shortstop Blas Monaco. He recalled, "I remember that early morning following the loss to Syracuse and getting the news of the fire. I was sound asleep when the phone rang about four in the morning. It was Herb Armstrong, our general manager. He said, 'Blas, I have bad news for you. Oriole Park has burned down. I don't know when we will be able to play again. It's awful.' I said, 'No, Herb, it's good. I'm having a lousy year.'"

Henry Walker, of 2927 North Calvert Street, cultivates his Victory Garden during a wartime summer. Out of patriotism, and in some measure to ensure their own personal supply of vegetables and to avoid standing in line at grocery stores, residents young and old began to dig and cultivate Victory Gardens. So popular were they that radio station WFBR aired a program of encouragement, advice, and recognition, "The Victory Garden of the Air."

and, as Mr. Pusin remembered the occasion, celebrated with mixed feelings. "We were happy to see the attack was under way, but we knew that after the soldiers got beyond the beaches the German resistance would stiffen and a lot of American soldiers were going to die." News that some already had was not long in coming.

George Wills, then eight years old, lived out McDonogh Road. He remembers his father, who taught at McDonogh School, awakening the family at 5:00 a.m. on June 6. It was for the boy a powerful experience and his first memory of the war. "I am going to turn on the radio," his father said. "Listen to our president."

A week later the McDonogh headmaster, Louis Lamborn (a World War I cavalry major; all the students called him "Doc"), "called a special assembly at the school and read the names of the McDonogh graduates who had died in the invasion—each name followed by a tolling of the chapel bell, just a few hundred feet away from the assembly room. All of us 'cadets' (McDonogh was a military school then) stood at attention in uniform and saluted as Major Lamborn read each name. All were familiar to many of us; the roll call included two sons of a teacher, both killed on Omaha Beach."

Hope to see one every week!

The featured photo in each issue of the Service edition of the *Sun* was always "cheesecake" on display—a bathing beauty clad in what for the era was "thinly." The picture for July 9, 1944, was typical: "Motion picture star Marguerite Chapman wearing one of the newer sarong-type, tie-on beach outfits to be seen at Maryland resorts."

The *Sun* described its Service edition as "a miniature hometown newspaper designed for mailing to Marylanders now serving in the Armed Forces of the United States." "Miniature" meant four pages at 7 × 9 inches. It appeared in the *Sunday Sun Magazine* as a "clip-out." It could be folded and mailed in any standard-size envelope.

The Service edition used a three-column format and dependably formulaic content. The right-hand two columns on page 1 always featured what was thought to be the big news locally: "City Blackout Successful," "Jackson Gets Fifth Term Bid," "Orioles Win," etc. Inside, the paper delivered several photos of goings-on about town, a cartoon by the *Sun*'s Richard Q. Yardley, and letters from servicemen expressing their appreciation of the paper. No sooner had the first edition appeared in early summer 1942 than a grateful and appreciative reader, Mrs. A. E. Knott, wrote in to say thanks. She said she had a son overseas and would forward it to him. "Hope to see one every week!"

Sometimes the *Sun* reported deliberately homey events—or so it seems in retrospect. A city forester, according to a mid-war story, wearing spiked shoes and equipped with a rope, visited 4000 Carlisle Avenue in Forest Park. Why? To persuade Carolyn Noll's pet cat to come out of a tree. She'd been up there four days.

They could be in Burma or London, Guadalcanal or Bastogne, North Africa or Sicily—wherever Maryland's soldiers, sailors, marines, and airmen served—and if they wondered what was going on back in the old home town, they could read all about it in the Service edition of the *Baltimore Sun*. (It survived until mid-February 1947.)

Baltimore's mouth-watering watermelons

As dawn lit up the waterfront area around Pratt and Market Place, known as Long Dock, the scene that came to life was warmly familiar to Baltimoreans in that prewar and war time: Dozens of working boats (bugeyes, skipjacks, and schooners) tied to the piers, some of them two and three across. Even this early, before the sun was up, crowds milled about on the docks and on the boats themselves. They were here to buy watermelons, homegrown in the Eastern Shore's Talbot, Dorchester, and Queen Anne's counties.

In the 1940s there were few supermarkets, and roadside stands were distant and more difficult to get to. The most popular way for a knowing Baltimorean to get his watermelon was to visit Long Dock at daybreak of any given day in July or August. "Half of Baltimore," Capt. Homer Pruitt, who owned one of those working boats, would recall years later, "seemed to be down at the Long Dock buying watermelons." The buyers, many of them wholesale fruit and vegetable merchants who later that same day would resell the melons to restaurants and A-rabs (Baltimore's storied horse and wagon hucksters), would go from boat to boat, inspecting, sampling, bargaining for the best buy, responding to the salesmanship of each captain-turned-hawker. "Come aboard, friend, come aboard. Sweet, red, and ripe. Congo! Georgie Rattlesnakes! Watermelons! Watermelons!"

The high point of confrontation—buyer-to-seller, for one melon or a hundred—was the moment the captain "plugged" a melon and let the skeptical buyer taste a sample. (People who remember the experience say a "plugged" melon was a "sold" melon!) On a day in 1944, among those moving boat to boat, tasting plug after plug, was fourteen-year-old Henry Lanasa, the fourth generation in his family of watermelon buyers to taste those juicy plugs. Years later, in his sixties, he said that his boyhood experiences of buying watermelons at Long Dock were still vivid for him. "I would go there with my father and my grandfather," he said. "We'd go boat to boat, walking from one to the other. The captains knew we were big buyers, so they'd turn on the hard sell. 'Best of the season' they'd say. 'No sense shopping around, you can't beat these.' There'd be people from as far away as Philadelphia—and a lot of shouting and bustling, lots of trucks and wagons in a mess of snarled traffic all around the Market Place area. Streetcars had to fight their way through the confusion.

"And, yes, thinking back, one reason for buying watermelons at

August 1944, a typically hot and humid month in Baltimore. Workers at Glenn L. Martin, quartered in the dense and crowded trailer parks, took to the beaches at the nearby Middle River for a much-needed and cooling break from wartime routine.

In the fall of 1944, more than a quarter of all employees taking the Victory Ship electrical course at Bethlehem-Fairfield shipyards were women. This group, photographed on September 7, 1944, learns electric-light wiring and communications systems by means of a wiring panel. "When a wrong connection is made," according to instructions, "the bulb lights up."

Long Dock during the war was that for all the fruits and vegetables grown in the Victory Gardens in those days, almost nobody was growing watermelons. So we had the watermelon market for ourselves."

Despite having lost clubhouse and home stands in July 1944, the Baltimore Orioles went on to win the International League championship that season—the first for the team since 1925. Celebrants in this photograph included Howie Moss, Pat Riley, Milton Stockhausen, Hal Kleine, Manager Tommy Thomas, Stan Benjamin, Bob Latshaw, Lou Kahn, Ken Braun, Stan West, Harry Imhoff, Red Embree, Frankie Skaff, George Hooks, Sam Lowry, Frank Rochevot, Johnny Podgajny, Felix Mackiewicz, Trainer Weidner, Fred Pfeifer, George Shaefer, Ambrose Palica, Rollie Van Slate, Sherman Lollar, and Blas Monaco.

Just prior to the game, in the divisional race, the Newark Bears had a winning mark of .559, six points ahead of the Birds, at .553. By the end of the day, the race was over. Final standings:

	Won	Lost	%
Orioles	84	68	.5526
Newark	85	69	.5519

The Orioles' winning margin of .0007 seems to have been the closest margin in league history. Twenty-five thousand fans greeted the team when their train arrived at Penn Station that night, Sunday, September 10—crowding the concourse, the stairs, the track-level platforms, and even the tracks.

The *Sun* reported: "Fans stood on benches, on windowsills, baggage trucks and radiators. Gov. Herbert R. O'Conor and Mayor Theodore R. McKeldin were there. The mayor had in his pocket two 'keys to the city' to present to Tommy Thomas and Stan Benjamin, Orioles manager and captain, respectively. But he never got a chance to present them.

"In a corner of the station, the crowd spotted young Jack Dunn, third owner of the Orioles, who received his wings as a second lieutenant in the AAF the previous day. He was still giving autographs an hour later. Outside, the streets for blocks were jammed with parked cars. Traffic came to a standstill from time to time. There was backslapping and loud happy talk and enthusiasm that hadn't been seen here in many a day. Parades began everywhere near the station. Baltimore had waited a long time for the chance and made the most of it."

"The cry was out," Efrem Potts recalled. "On to Louisville!"

The Orioles went on to win the Junior World series, defeating Louisville four games to two. On October 11 the *Sun* reported, "The season had seen the greatest resurgence of baseball enthusiasm in Baltimore in 20 years."

Food shortages meant waiting in lines, like this one on October 19, 1944. Mrs. Louise Reynolds remembered standing in those lines. "To me, rationing, *rationing,* was among the most discomforting problems of wartime in Baltimore. That, and the blackouts. I remember those ration books—everything seemed to be rationed. Coffee, and tea in particular, seemed hard to get. I'd stand in line in Lexington Market to get a roast—once in a while we could get beef or pork. Chicken was easy to get, because, I guess, we raised a lot of them locally. You had to have a good relationship with your grocer. I did. You always had to have coupons. Always, always there were the ration coupons...I remember one dinner party we went to the hostess served toasted rolls topped with cheese, with sliced hardboiled eggs on top, and a sauce over all of it. I think back on that dish with joy—it was so good."

Maybe we should have had to make some sacrifices, but honestly, we didn't

Catherine "Kat" Ketron Fletcher was twenty-four and living with her parents at 1125 St. Paul Street when war broke out. "The house had five floors. My father, a doctor, had his offices on the first floor, and we lived on the second, third, and fourth. We had three servants, and they lived on the fifth. I knew there was a war on, but we didn't seem to feel it. I don't recall that we ever wanted for anything.

"The truth about life in wartime Baltimore, as I remember it, is that sacrifice was uneven and inequitable, and some, with money and connections, didn't sacrifice at all. This was a group that lived during the war pretty much as they did before, and after it. I really don't know how we and our friends managed that, but we did. Maybe we should

A wartime Halloween dance at the 305 West Monument Street USO, with shocks of corn and pumpkins everywhere, Japanese lanterns hanging overhead, and hostesses in gay costumes—a welcomed night away from the army and navy.

have had to make some sacrifices, but honestly, we didn't. That's just the way it was for some Baltimoreans."

The Baltimoreans Ms. Fletcher was talking about had all the sugar and hosiery and gasoline and hard-to-get Scotch whisky they needed. "We all owned summer homes on Gibson Island, and the closest some of us got to the war was teaching the kids out there to wrap bandages for the Red Cross. We played golf, with the take going to Bundles for Britain.

"My father and I were air-raid wardens—that was a joke. Once during a drill we found ourselves during our rounds wearing gas masks and trying to make our way to the command post, which was supposed to be a few blocks away. But all of the streets were dark; there was no light anywhere, and we kept hugging the curb to make our way. We found ourselves in Curtis Bay.

"I worked nine to five, no shifts, no lunch boxes, and no overalls,

The reading room of the USO at 339 North Charles Street supplied a comfortable place to read the latest war news. The *Sun* of November 10, 1944, reported on the Allied offensive in southern France.

in neat and clean surroundings. The company was the Koppers American Hammered Piston Ring Division, and I had a very responsible job. I had to master the techniques of a very sophisticated process to determine if piston rings were of the exact strength they needed to be for use in the production of armaments. I was officially a 'spectrographer.'

"My family never seemed to suffer from shortages of anything. My father had a large practice in dermatology and a wide circle of colleagues from Johns Hopkins, and we all had cars and we all gave parties at one another's houses and we all drove to where we wanted to go. I remember my mother coming back from the North Avenue Market loaded down with the best meats. I don't remember the war as a time of loss or sacrifice. Somehow, and I will never know, my family and our friends went through the war without the sense that we *were* at war.

"I'm not defending all of that, it's just the way it was.

"For some of us, anyway."

Life was good if you could be a WAVE stationed at the Bainbridge Naval Training Center in Cecil County, Maryland, on Thanksgiving, 1944.

The Gold Street USO, at Gold and
Brunt streets, one of three canteens
for African American servicemen.

The Gold Street USO Planning Committee at work. "Negro servicemen who visit the Gold Street USO Club," explained the *Afro-American* on December 15, 1944, "are encouraged to display their talents and interests.

"Several programs are presented for the boys. Thirty soldiers, as members of the Java Club, are responsible for the religious program on Sunday morning known as 'devotions.' Each week they choose one of their number to lead the hymn singing and the responsive reading and to say his favorite prayer.

"Because the servicemen are constantly being transferred from one camp to another, the Java Club is a rather loose organization. A women's auxiliary, led by Mrs. Tazewell A. Johnson, of 2309 Madison Avenue, arranges for the serving of breakfast by different church or community groups. Fred S. A. Johnson is director of the club.

"The church talent group sends soldiers into churches to speak, sing, and play the organ, with the result that civilians and members of the armed forces have come to a better understanding.

"Cultural programs and voice recordings provide further outlets for talents. Most of the boys want to record conversations for their mothers and sweethearts. These are censored and mailed by the USO.

"The Gold Street Club building, which was originally a fire-engine house, is described by Mr. Johnson as 'substantial, with character.' Evidence of its former state are three boarded-up holes in the ceilings, through which two brass poles and a circular iron staircase once passed.

"In September of 1942 remodelers started work on the structure. It was opened to visitors December 14 of the same year. The sloping cement floor had been leveled off and covered with linoleum. Gold, tan, and deep-red curtains were hung to match the leather covering of pale wood chairs.

"A large lounge with an information bureau, writing facilities, and a snack bar, where food and soft drinks are served at cost, are on the first floor. Above this are the game room, library, and ballroom. An outdoor play area behind the building has recently been completed.

"In the past year, thousands of soldiers have visited the club. They were entertained by 145 senior hostesses and 975 junior hostesses. Sunday is the busiest day, Saturday the busiest night. Monday and Friday evenings are very light.

"Games are an essential part of the USO program, according to Herbert F. Thompson, assistant director, who organized Ping-Pong tournaments, musical mixers, quiz programs, and scavenger hunts."

December 2, 1944: While fighting raged in battlefields in Europe and in the Pacific, the country took time out on a chilly Saturday afternoon to watch the Army-Navy football game in Baltimore's Municipal Stadium on Thirty-third Street. President Roosevelt and Secretary of the Treasury Henry Morgenthau Jr. were not about to let the country forget the war entirely: to get a ticket to the game, football fans had to buy war bonds.

Hotels and restaurants were overwhelmed with requests for accommodations. Thousands of passengers arrived by Baltimore & Ohio and Pennsylvania Railroad trains from New York, Philadelphia, and Washington. "Thousands of persons in trolleys, private automobiles, station wagons, busses and trucks and on foot," the *Sun* reported, "plus 5,600 marching cadets and midshipmen, moved on to Municipal Stadium, beginning at 10 a.m., to be in at the kickoff of the annual football extravaganza."

Joining them were recuperating servicemen from Walter Reed Hospital, Bethesda National Naval Medical Center, Fort Myer Hospital, Fort Howard Veterans Hospital, and the Curtis Bay Coast Guard Hospital.

Some seventy thousand people attended the game, braving the cold, among them Adm. William D. Leahy, naval aide to President Roosevelt and senior member of the joint chiefs of staff. In FDR's absence, Leahy carried out the presidential tradition of moving, at half time, from one side of the field to the other.

Final score: Army 23, Navy 7.

From his faraway base in the Pacific, Gen. Douglas MacArthur, a former superintendent of West Point, cabled Col. Earl H. "Red" Blaik, West Point head coach: "WE HAVE STOPPED THE WAR TO CELEBRATE YOUR MAGNIFICENT SUCCESS."

The navy may have lost the game that day in Baltimore in 1944, but in the war-bond effort the United States of America came out big winners: the game raised nearly $60 million.

★ ★ ★ VICTORY

In early summer 1944, the Allies had invaded the continent of Europe. Slightly less than a year later, on May 8, 1945, Germany surrendered (V-E Day), and downtown Baltimore enjoyed a delirious dance in a rain of confetti. But the war in the Pacific ground on, shortages continued, and the dreaded telegrams ("We regret to inform you...") kept arriving. Not until mid-August, after thousands more U.S. casualties and the dawn of a new age in the science of mass killing did Japan surrender, releasing a torrent of joy at home (as well as on U.S. ships and bases in the Pacific). The war, after four years, was over—over there and over here. Thousands paraded and danced in the streets. At long last, home front Baltimore was on the way back to becoming hometown Baltimore.

Winter of '45

During the week beginning Monday, February 19, Baltimoreans learned that American troops were landing on Iwo Jima, and they read on the society pages of the Sunpapers and the *News-Post* of several Baltimore debutantes' weddings, replete with pictures. Baltimoreans who lacked invitations need not have felt left out; they could have gone to some great movies: *Earl Carroll's Vanities* at the Hippodrome; *Keys of the Kingdom* at the New; *Dark Waters* at the Century, *Meet Me in St. Louis* at the Valencia. They might also have taken in the Club Charles (Charles and Preston), where a newcomer was trying to make it as a solo act, a crooner named Dean Martin. Before the month was out, they saw something in their newspapers stirring and memorable— U.S. Marines raising the Stars and Stripes at Iwo Jima.

Top, Gen. George C. Marshall, Chief of Staff of the United States Army and soon to be awarded five-star rank, signs autographs for fans at the Army-Navy game in Baltimore, December 2, 1944.

Right, The No. 6 streetcar was an especially popular line; it started in East Baltimore and took passengers west, into and through downtown, and then turned south to the shipyards and defense plants along Key Highway and in Curtis Bay. Jerry Kelly, a historian at the Baltimore Streetcar Museum, said, "When the shifts changed, the streetcars were running so close to one another, so tightly packed front to back, that you could walk along the roofs of the cars, skipping car to car, for the length of a full city block."

Top, President Roosevelt died in Warm Springs, Georgia, on Thursday, April 12, 1945. His funeral train passed through Baltimore on the evening of the following Saturday (April 14), past crowds that had gathered along the route to pay a silent and final tribute. The build-up started as early as 7:00 p.m., although the funeral train was not expected until eleven that night. When the train made its way into the city, it moved slowly through Arbutus and under the Wilkens Avenue bridge, then north under the Edmondson Avenue bridge. There were two trains; the first consisted of fourteen cars, the second of twelve. The rear section of the final car in the second train was lighted; in it was the casket, draped in an American flag and plainly visible. At each of the four corners a uniformed serviceman stood at attention, forming an honor guard.

The train did not stop in Penn Station. There was no ceremony. But Mayor McKeldin (pictured, *lower left*) and other officials were there on the platform, forming a reception of quiet respect.

Right, Standing by the tracks were Congressman Thomas D'Alesandro Jr. and, kept close, his twelve-year-old son, Franklin D. Roosevelt D'Alesandro, born on March 7, 1933—three days after the then newly elected president's first of four inaugurations.

In mid-April the *Sun* ran an article featuring the sisters Marie Holthause and Edna Holthause, both of whom had served for years as junior hostesses and dancers at the USO on North Charles Street and were eager to reminisce. Marie said, "These soldiers, sailors and marines come from every state in the union, and we have learned to adapt to the dancing styles peculiar to the part of the country the servicemen come from." Edna said, "Virginia guys can be identified by their wrigglin'. They always have their legs in a knot. Men from Pennsylvania have a passion for pivoting." Both sisters agreed that the "gobs from New York and Chicago have it all over those from the rest of the country, when it comes to learning new routines."

They were of one mind that New York, Pennsylvania, and Chicago servicemen are "big talkers." Marie insisted that she could always tell when a New York guy lives in Brooklyn, "because if he does, he tells you right away."

The girls wore out a pair of shoes, they said, in two or three weeks. "Our ration stamps don't provide us with enough shoes," Edna explained. "So when they wear out from dancing, we buy un-rationed shoes. They have synthetic rubber soles. Great for jitterbugging."

Last dance at the Summit

"It was a big old sprawling mansion out Old Pimlico Road," Sig Brothman recalls, "with four large rooms, a center hallway, and a wide front porch." Mr. Brothman's father, Joseph, bought the house in 1923 and converted its first floor into a nightclub and called it the Summit. He moved his family onto the second floor, which is where Sig grew up.

Living upstairs from the nightclub, young Sig got to hear, coming from downstairs, some of the best big-band music ever played in America. He recalled, "Guy Lombardo played the Summit in 1931. Isham Jones and Stan Kenton came through, too, on the way to prominence. So did, as part of the Ben Pollack band, Glenn Miller and the Dorsey brothers. I remember one summer night in 1939. Louis Prima was playing. We probably had seven hundred people out there, and I mean *out* there—Pimlico Road was a one-lane gravel track out into the wilderness. It was a lovely scene. The trees around the porch were rigged with colored lights. Inside, people were dancing to Louis Prima's orchestra—a lot of lively songs with an Italian tarantella rhythm. Fantastic stuff."

Newly minted army second lieutenants Norvell Miller and Gerhart Schmeisner were at the Summit with their dates on a night in mid-April 1945. Norvell recalled, "I know it was shortly after President Roosevelt died, because our travel orders got shuffled about. It was a really neat place to go to dance—festive, with a big dance floor, and lots of danceable music. In those wartime years, for a soldier and his date, the Summit was *the* place to be, crowded with army and navy officers and enlisted men, some dancing their last dance for the duration."

The Summit was open only from spring through fall. It closed sometime after the war.

Many a couple—a serviceman far from home with his date—danced and celebrated at the Summit on many a night in those wartime years, but Sig Brothman, recalling the times years later, said he thinks he missed most of it. "Listening in bed upstairs," he said, "I always fell asleep."

Miss Dorothy Stanley read "The American Way"

Throughout that same spring, while a nation was mourning the death of its Great Depression and wartime leader, American troops in the Pacific continued to be engaged in the costly and bloody battle for the island of Okinawa. In Europe, on April 11, American forces liberated

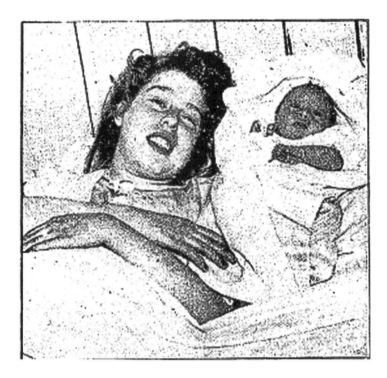

As news of the German surrender crackled on radios around the world, Mrs. John Helm, of 603 South Hanover Street, was in hard labor at Volunteers for America hospital. She delivered a beautiful baby girl that May 7, naming her *Victoria Europa.*

Buchenwald concentration camp; on April 15, a British-Canadian unit, Bergen-Belsen; on April 29, American forces liberated Dachau. Back in Baltimore, in these same sunny April days, the residents of Mount Vernon Place were vigorously protesting against a newly issued city ordinance banishing dogs from the squares.

On Monday morning, May 7, in a light rain, the news spread quickly through the city that Germany had surrendered. Recognition of the historic moment was not long in coming; pictured, showers of confetti swirling down from the upper floors of downtown buildings. Office workers streamed out into the streets, four and five arm in arm, skipping and cheering. By mid-afternoon the rain had stopped, and the celebration appeared to be, suddenly, subdued—people seemed on second thought to understand down deep that the war was over only in Europe and that they were caught in a half-celebration. Everyone understood: The war in the Pacific was grinding on—victory was not final. Loved ones were still being reported missing. Or killed. For victory to be final, there needed to be one more.

But there was now a need, long pent up, to celebrate *something,* and by mid-afternoon crowds were milling about the sidewalks and overflowing into the streets, embracing one another, waving American flags, halting traffic. Though many were wearing V-E buttons purchased

Here the height of V-E Day merriment in front of the Baltimore and Ohio Railroad building at Baltimore and Charles streets.

from well-stocked and ready-for-business sidewalk vendors, the official V-E announcement would not come until the next morning, Tuesday, May 8, when President Harry S Truman addressed the nation.

Baltimore's public schools remained in session on V-E Day, but all celebrated by listening to broadcast announcements from President Truman and Prime Minister Churchill and discussing the significance of the victory in Europe. The *Afro-American* reported on its reception at the "colored" schools:

"The sophomore class of Coppin Normal School dramatized the end of the National Anthem, after which the students gave their attitudes toward the war. Miss Sarah Welsh presided and Mrs. Grace Jacobs, teacher of social sciences, sponsored the program. Dr. Miles Connor is principal.

Several young ladies, workers in the downtown office buildings, leapt outside to celebrate on May 8.

"Dunbar High School held its program on Monday. Luther Mitchell, history teacher, spoke on causes of the war, and Mrs. Vivian Cook, vice principal, summarized the reactions of the women of the world toward victory. W. T. Cain spoke for the young people and Carrington L. Davis, principal, talked on the significance of the victory. The school also assembled Tuesday morning, to hear the broadcast.

"Douglass High School honored its 800 boys in the armed forces during its V-E day program. Tributes were given by Misses Pearl Sewell, Ethel Cherry, Peggy Campbell, Ella Taveres and Barbara Jones. Miss Dorothy Stanley read 'The American Way,' and the eleventh and twelfth grades male chorus sang."

"I missed the V-E day celebration," Bob Rappaport said, "I found out about it while I was on the train to Atlantic City. We stopped at Philadelphia and a few people got on and told all of the passengers that the Germans had just surrendered."

Everyone seemed to understand that the war in the Pacific was continuing, and casualties would be heavy, and there was a butcher's bill yet to be paid.

Right, Sun Square revelry on V-E Day.

Bottom, On the afternoon of May 8 a long, colorful, and noisy V-E victory parade wound its way through the streets of Baltimore. The Holy Name Society band led the way.

Amid the noise and hoopla and falling confetti of the V-E Day celebration in downtown Baltimore, a *Sun* photographer noticed a young man in civilian clothes, sitting by himself on the window ledge of a building and taking in the news of the German surrender while looking alternately at a map of Europe, as if trying to make sense of the news. To the photographer, the young man appeared to have a strong interest in, and even knowledge of, the news, but he would tell the photographer only that he was a "discharged veteran." He would not give his name, nor would he discuss his service record or his seeming familiarity with the turn of events in Europe, leaving the photographer to wonder...

One hundred men of Maryland and the District of Columbia remembered May 8, 1945, not only because it was V-E Day but also because it was the day they were sworn into the U.S. Army. The ceremony took place at the Fifth Regiment Armory. Then the inductees marched off the drill floor, out the main entrance, and into buses that took them to Penn Station, where they boarded a train that would take them to Fort Meade. For them, the war was just beginning. Inductee Walter A. List, 30, of 342 South Fulton Avenue, recognized the situation. He said, "The job of beating Japan has got to be done. I will never forget V-E Day, you can be sure of that!"

The snack bar at the USO at 339 North Charles offered quick and pretty reasonable refreshments: "2 Do-Nuts" and "all the coffee you can drink" for five cents. Advertising sign on the mirror features a long-time, made-in-Baltimore ice cream, Hendler's.

I was attached to that flag, and so I took it home with me

When the war broke out, Charlotte Shenk was married, living at 4234 Shamrock Avenue and raising two young children. "My husband was exempt from the draft because of the work he was doing for Standard Oil, but we were very much involved with the war on the home front, through several of the Catholic institutions that provided support for the servicemen. We helped in hosting servicemen at the Shrine of the Little Flower, the Catholic Daughters of America, Knights of Columbus, and especially in the Catholic-sponsored USO in the Odd Fellows Hall at Cathedral and Saratoga streets.

"We volunteered there several days every week, and among my other duties, I was in charge of bringing and setting up on the stage a large American flag. It was maybe four feet by three feet, and somebody had sewn the letters *U S O* across one of the stripes. Well, the flag was there with me through all of the war years. Through the dances, the dinners, the many conversations we had with the boys far from home, and dearly in need of someone to talk to, and maybe make a call home with them.

"I have a lot of fond memories of those wartime days and nights in that USO on Saratoga Street. But when the war was over, so was my volunteering there, though that USO unit continued to serve the boys in peacetime.

"But I was attached to that flag, and so I took it home with me, and kept it, as a souvenir of a very special time in Baltimore and in my life. From 1945 through 2001—fifty-six years! I kept that flag furled in my home. It was linked to my memories of the USO and the war—not just my days and nights at that USO, but the rationing and the black-outs, and I have a vivid memory of how we prepared our meals during times of food shortages. On Shamrock Avenue, if you didn't have an ingredient you needed in your cooking, you went to a neighbor and traded her for something she needed and did not have. And the terrible scarcity of apartments and houses and places to live!

"After my husband died I moved into Charlestown in 1993 and in a painful downsizing, I had to give the flag away—after some fifty years of my attachment to it. It's now in the hands of the Disabled Veterans of America.

"But I think about that flag every now and then. So many memories of my life in Baltimore in wartime stay wrapped up in it…still."

It was all very confusing, with much hairsplitting and differing perspectives

Reuben Shiling worked for the Office of Price Administration, "popularly, or really un-popularly, known as the OPA. Our offices were located in the O'Sullivan Building—on the southwest corner of Light and Baltimore streets. And we were fighting a war of our own. It seemed that most everybody was in violation, wittingly or unwittingly, of the price controls set in place by the government.

"This war—the Maryland office of the OPA in continuing battle with the retailers, manufacturers, wholesalers, and consumers—broke out on Wednesday, May 6, 1942. On that day, newspaper ads alerted the public that when the stores opened Monday morning each would have on display its ceiling prices of every cost-controlled item. There would be hundreds of these items. Ceiling prices in all cases were limited to the highest price charged for each item as of March 30, 1942.

"You can imagine the confusion. Among the items that came under price control were almost every processed food—bread and bakery goods, beef, pork, sugar, milk and cream, ice cream, canned soups and fish, cereals, shortening, coffee, and tea. A long list.

"Also clothes, shoes, soap, fuel, cigarettes, drugs, toiletries. And furniture and furnishings, and appliances. The price of aspirin was frozen at fifteen cents; a can of spaghetti at fifteen cents; a large can of salmon, fifteen cents.

"It was an extremely complicated program to police. There were

The Office of Price Administration chart, with its confusing and hairsplitting rules.

so many violations and cases to be processed, we could barely keep up with them.

"At one point, in 1944, according to our records, as many as 68 percent of all retail grocers were violating the price-control laws, and 483 stores were overcharging for butter, 500 for top round beef, 300 for soap and corn flakes. And strangely enough, one of the major department stores was overcharging for their Kraft paper shopping bags! Over two thousand were oversold, for a total of $47.04.

"A housewife called to complain that her grocer was forcing coffee

On August 6, 1945, the B-29 *Enola Gay* dropped the world's first atomic bomb on the city of Hiroshima and changed the history of the war and the world. Baltimorean Lt. Jacob Beser was the radarman. Then, a few days later, on August 9, a second atomic bomb was dropped, this one on Nagasaki. By mid-August, Japanese defeats at Iwo Jima and Okinawa and the unrelenting heavy bombing of Japanese cities were taking their toll. Rumors of impending Japanese surrender circulated, and many of them found their way into the newspapers. Cpl. Bernard Silverstein, Lt. Norbourne Thomas, and Sgt. Albert Karl Sapp read the news that there is no news—so far. Behind them sit John P. Matusiewski and Philip Walston.

buyers to purchase, along with scarce coffee, a certain amount of other less-scarce goods. The practice was so widespread it had a name—'tie-in agreements.' Another complainant said that she had purchased one and a quarter pounds of lamb chops and was charged for them at the rate of forty-four cents a pound when the ceiling was forty-two cents.

"A mother asked if it were proper for a department store to charge her a dollar extra for the cap to a child's snowsuit. She claimed that although the price of the suit hadn't been changed, the cap was formerly included. Another complained that a confectioner was charging sixteen cents extra for chocolate sauce that was formerly included in the price of a quart of ice cream.

"It was all very confusing, with much hairsplitting and differing perspectives.

"The war for the army and navy was over in August of 1945. But our war wasn't over until the day the OPA office closed in November of 1946.

"Ours was the longer war."

In the days after the bombing of Hiroshima and Nagasaki, many Americans expected Japan to capitulate, thus avoiding casualties on a scale military experts said would be horrific. Others believed the Japanese capable of putting up the suicidal resistance they had demonstrated on both Iwo and Okinawa—on a scale hundreds of times larger. A great many Baltimoreans thought to hurry along the surrender and savings in lives with prayer. On August 9, 1945, after hearing of the bombing of Nagasaki (a heavily Roman Catholic city), these meditative Catholics gathered for a service at Saint Alphonsus Church, at 114 West Saratoga Street.

On August 10, rumors spread that the Japanese had made an offer of surrender, and by 7:00 a.m. local time the switchboards of the *Sun, News-Post, Afro-American,* and City Hall were swamped with inquiries. Mrs. Elaine Steiner, 3410 Guilford Avenue, remained cautious, reported the *Sun* two days later, "expressing the mood of hesitancy." "I got stung on the announcement on V-E Day," she explained, "and I am just going to wait for the real thing this time." Police Commissioner Joseph Wallace, determined not to be caught napping if peace broke out, placed some two thousand officers on alert in case of V-J Day. Late in the afternoon and into the early evening of Tuesday, August

14, a growing and impatient crowd gathered in Sun Square. They kept their eyes focused upwards at the *Sun's* faithful Trans Lux news ticker, watching the bulletins as they moved across in lights, waiting for the final word ("Japan Surrenders!") after days of false rumor.

President Truman's official announcement finally came from Washington early Tuesday evening, and the dam broke. Cheers went up, there was dancing in the streets. Baltimoreans by the thousands rushed downtown, equipped with noisemakers, cowbells, flags, horns, and bags of confetti. As the celebrations grew larger and noisier, the servicemen who happened to be in Baltimore this night had a field

day. A soldier grabbed a young woman around the waist and said, "I came all the way from Oklahoma to get a kiss from you!" "Help yourself," she said. When he did, the crowd roared.

War plants closed, traffic stopped dead in the center of the city, thousands went to church to offer prayers of thanksgiving.

This photograph captures Sun Square, looking east along East Baltimore Street.

"I learned the news as I was driving downtown," later recalled Mrs. Louisa Reynolds, who had found the air-raid sirens especially frightening. "I heard it on the car radio. I tell you, joy coursed through me. I was so thrilled! So thrilled!"

Weather Forecast
Considerable cloudiness and continued warm today, with showers in afternoon. Yesterday's temperatures: Highest, 85; lowest, 74; mean, 80............Page 17

THE SUN FINAL

Registered United States Patent Office

Vol. 217—No. 77—F | PAID CIRCULATION JULY MORNING, 175,213 EVENING, 190,130 365,343 || SUNDAY 275,960 | BALTIMORE, WEDNESDAY, AUGUST 15, 1945 | Entered as second-class matter at Baltimore Post Office | Zone 3 | 18 Pages | 3 Cents

THE WAR IS OVER

BIG CUT IN DRAFT CALL; 2-DAY WORK HOLIDAY; MANPOWER CURBS END

Truman Foresees Release Of 5 Million GI's; Induction Of Men Over 25 Ordered Halted; Navy Cuts Nearly 6 Billion In Contracts

Truman forecasts release of 5,000,000 soldiers.
President sets today and tomorrow as holidays.
U. S. revokes all wartime manpower controls.
Navy cancels nearly $6,000,000,000 in contracts.
Congress will reconvene on September 5.

Washington, Aug. 14 (AP)—President Truman tonight forecast that 5,000,000 to 5,500,000 men now in the Army may be returned to civilian life within the next twelve to eighteen months.

Furthermore, he said in announcing Japan's surrender, only the lowest age groups will now be drafted into the Army. Preliminary estimates indicate only those under 26 will be called, Mr. Truman added.

Urges Cut In Inductions

His recommendation was that selective service reduce inductions immediately from 80,000 a month to 50,000.

Maj. Gen. Lewis B. Hershey, selective service director, following Mr. Truman's instuctions, tonight telegraphed all state directors ordering them to stop at once the induction of all registrants 26 years of age or older.

"It is too early to propose a definite figure for the occupation forces which will be required in the Pacific twelve months from now or what reduction it may be possible to make in the strength of the army force now allotted to occupation duties in Europe," the President said in a statement.

"It is apparent, however, that we can release as many men as can be brought home by the means available during the next year."

Army releases will be speeded by air and sea transportation in an effort to attain that 5,000,000 to 5,500,000 figure, he said.

Mr. Truman said that, in justice to millions of men who have given "long and faithful service under the difficult and hazardous conditions of the Pacific war and elsewhere overseas, a constant flow of replacements to the occupational forces is thought to be imperative."

He added that inductions of 50,000 a month in the lowest age groups "will provide only sufficient men to support the forces required for occupational duty and to permit the relief of long-service men overseas to the maximum extent transportation makes possible."

Present Problem Cited

The present problem, he said, centers on the readjustment of personnel now in uniform and induction of new men through selective service to "permit the earliest possible release from the Army of those men who have long records of dangerous, arduous and faithful service."

The President did not mention the Navy draft call, currently about 20,000 men a month.

General Hershey said he had no word of the Navy's plans, but that it would be "reasonable to expect a cut there, too."

Actually men through 37 previously were subject to the draft, but in practice the calls the last few months have been confined to men under 30.

Hershey said he regarded the President's instructions "as a flat prohibition" on drafting of men 26 and over.

President Proclaims Holidays

Washington, Aug. 14 (AP)—Tomorrow and Thursday are legal holidays and days off for Government workers, and holidays for pay purposes for workers in general.

And V-J day, when it comes, will be a premium pay day, too.

President Truman announced both rulings tonight.

He directed agency heads throughout the Government to cut their forces down to a bare skeleton staff August 15 and 16 and not to charge the two days against the employes' annual leave.

"Inadequate" Recognition

He said it was in "inadequate" recognition of the four-year efforts of "one of the hardest-working groups of war workers."

For other workers under wage control, Wednesday and Thursday count like Christmas and the few other accepted holidays for purposes of overtime pay and in figuring the number of days worked in a week. Many employers already have gotten approval for regular-time pay to workers who take the day off.

Postal service for the next two days will "approximate holiday service," the Post Office Department said.

V-J Day Holiday Expected

Local postmasters will have wide discretion in carrying out the President's wishes, it was indicated, and those postal employés required to work tomorrow and the next day will have compensating time off at a later date.

It was presumed, but not specifically stated, that government workers generally will be off on V-J day, too.

The White House said the next two days are to be regarded as legal holidays.

Navy Drops 6 Billions In Orders

Washington, Aug. 14 (AP)—The Navy announced tonight it is canceling nearly $6,000,000,000 in prime contracts.

This is in addition to a recently announced $1,200,000,000 cut in the shipbuilding program.

The cancellations were ordered, the Navy said, to bring production into line with requirements of the postwar navy and to free men, materials and productive capacity for manufacture of civilian goods.

Some Orders To Remain

Many types of procurement will be reduced in percentage, the Navy said, with some orders remaining on the books.

Large numbers of aircraft scheduled for production will be cut back, together with engines and propellers. However, as long as the fleet is kept at its present size, a certain number of replacement planes must be procured.

Since it is no longer necessary to maintain munitions stocks at war levels, cuts were ordered in procurement of ordnance materials—particularly projectiles, explosives, bombs, mines and torpedoes.

Other Ordnance To Be Cut

Other ordnance also will be cut, but production will be maintained on items required for vessels under construction or repair, and for research and experimental work.

Large shipbuilding cutbacks have already been announced, but other reductions are being made in components for ships, propulsion machinery and spare parts.

Preparation has been under way for several months for termination of navy contracts with the war's end.

Manpower Controls Revoked

Washington, Aug. 14 (AP)—The Government today revoked all wartime manpower controls, effective immediately, and set forth a plan aimed at speedy re-employment of veterans and released war workers.

In an action timed to coincide with Japan's surrender, the War Manpower Commission announced a seven-point program which it said would stimulate "reconversion activities and the speedy re-employment of displaced workers, at the same time restoring a free labor market."

48-Hour Week Out

Among the controls lifted are those providing for hiring through the United States Employment Service, employment ceilings to channel workers to essential industries and the requirement for certificates of availability in changing jobs.

Eliminated also was the mandatory feature of the 48-hour week in areas or industry where it is in effect, an official said. However, the Little Steel formula for general wage stabilization is not affected by the action of the WMC, which has no jurisdiction over it.

Specific Provisions

Frank L. McNamee, acting WMC chairman, said regional directors have been instructed to put the new program into effect at once in

(Continued on Page 7, Column 2)

PEACE COMES TO BALTIMORE—Sun Square after proclamation of Japan's surrender.—Photo by LeRoy B. Merriken.

TORPEDO SINKS INDIANAPOLIS

883 Of Cruiser's Crew Lost; 315 Rescued After 5 Days

Peleliu, Palau Islands, Aug. 5 (AP—Delayed)—The 10,000-ton cruiser Indianapolis was sunk in less than fifteen minutes, presumably by a Japanese submarine, twelve minutes past midnight July 30—and 883 crew members lost their lives in one of the Navy's worst disasters.

She went down in the Philippine Sea, within 450 miles of Leyte, while on an unescorted high-speed run from San Francisco.

She had completed the trip to Guam and was bound for the Philippines.

Without A Second's Warning

There were 315 survivors.

[The Navy in Washington, first to announce the tragedy, said there were "100 per cent casualties" and listed 5 Navy dead, including one officer; 845 Navy missing, including 63 officers; 307 Navy wounded, including 15 officers; 30 Marine Corps missing, including 2 officers, and 9 enlisted Marine Corps wounded.]

The fatal torpedo attack came without a second's warning. Two explosions flashed out of her bow. She quivered while flames streaked down passageways all through her hull.

In less than fifteen minutes the Indianapolis was gone; 10,000 tons of "proud and happy" ship plunged headfirst into the sea.

315 Survive 5 Days In Sea

Nobody outside the oil-covered circle of men and debris in the water knew her fate until after a Peleliu search plane led the way to the rescue of the 315 men who survived five days in the sea.

Nearly 700 men went down with the ship. Hundreds more jumped off the cruiser's rearing side in time—but many were without life preservers or rafts, without clothing, without hope of remaining afloat for long.

Survivors believe two underwater torpedoes smashed into the starboard side near the bow of the 14-year-old cruiser, setting off one of the 8-inch gun magazines.

Radio Efforts Futile

Gun crews manned their stations and stayed there while the ship pitched over violently. Radiomen tried desperately to get out a message to all ships' stations—"Hit. Position longitude — latitude —. Need immediate assistance." But it was no use; the ship's power was dead and radio keys clicked futilely the words that might have saved hundreds of lives.

When the skipper, Capt. Charles Butler McVay 3d, of Washington, D.C., saw the badly listing ship was going fast, he had the "abandon ship" order passed by word of mouth through the darkened, fire-scaled compartments of the 610-foot ship.

What happened in the last 15 minutes aboard the Indianapolis was a living nightmare of flames, explosions, of men screaming, of others making near-miraculous escapes, of watching the one-time 5th Fleet flagship of Admiral Raymond A. Spruance founder helplessly, and disappear.

Spruance was not aboard when she was hit.

For the nearly 500 men who

(Continued on Page 3, Column 2)

Flood Of Joy Sweeps Through Allied World

Baltimore cuts loose with bang as 200,000 fill downtown streets to celebrate............Page 18

New York, Aug. 14 (AP)—A couple of false starts didn't dim New York's enthusiasm for celebrating victory tonight.

There were almost 500,000 persons—police figures—in Times Square when the announcement came. The noise then, with no particular provocation except the day's mounting tension, was so great that the blare of the news from a radio sound truck almost was drowned out. But the flashing lights of the bulletin board on the Times Annex Building told the story.

The tremendous roar that went up then made the previous clamor sound like the squeal of an ungreased axle. New York let loose with all the shenanigans for which it had trained since the first intimation last Friday that Japan was willing to talk peace.

Paper Salvage Drive Flouted

As in all celebrations in New York, paper cascaded from windows all over town. It came in streamers, in pieces, in packets, in rolls. It came in Chinatown, and in Harlem, in Little Italy and Hell's Kitchen, from Broadway to the Battery, in a midsummer snowstorm that covered the streets in an unmelting blanket which said nuts to the paper salvage drive.

The entire police department—14,000 men—was mobilized, as was the fire department. Mayor La Guardia was out in his radio patrol car when the news broke and even he promised himself "a couple of hours of relaxation and celebration." Then he hurried to a radio, proclaimed tomorrow and Thursday as victory holidays, and named Sunday as "world peace day" for giving thanks to God "for the complete victory."

On the East Side, in Little Italy, a barrage of firecrackers was loosed. On upper Broadway windows sprouted flags. Harbor boats set up a great din.

10 Cents For A Paper

On Forty-second street newsboys were getting 10 cents apiece for papers, the buyers seeking only tearing-up privileges. Chinatown brought out its sacred dragon, usually seen only in the Chinese New Year, and paraded with clashing cymbals, beating of drums, and popping firecrackers.

One thousand WAVES poured onto Broadway from their barracks at 76th street for a mass celebration. At 43d street, a sailor "shinnied" up a light pole. At Times Square, a Marine and a Brooklyn boy succeeded in raising a flag on the monument replica of the Iwo Jima picture. It was against regulations to raise a flag after sundown but officers told the two to go ahead.

Traffic was snarled. Motorists paid no attention to police and police paid no attention to motorists. Bars were busy but it was on the basis of in-for-a-quick-one-and-out-again. Some restaurants saw their customers gulp the last gulp of their coffee and race out the door without paying their checks.

Fire Hydrants Go On

On the East Side, celebrators devised a special trick of turning on fire hydrants. The same section saw a succession of bonfires in the streets. All the wounded men who could walk streamed out of the United States Veterans Hospital in The Bronx and stood at the gates in pajamas and bathrobes to cheer at civilians who cheered at them.

One temporary blank spot in the hubbub was the theaters. Managers did not announce the news of the surrender, fearing a stampede that might cause injuries.

Amid all the exuberance, though, there were many who turned their first thoughts to giving thanks to God. More than 2,500 attended a special victory mass at St. Patrick's Cathedral, just one hour after the Truman announcement. Other churches, too, held services but most of these were held off until Wednesday. The Fifth Avenue Presbyterian Church, for instance, announced hourly services from 11 A.M. through 5 P.M.

Building Up All Day

New York had been building up for the explosion all day. At noon, police figured there were 150,000 persons in Times Square, most of them just milling around. Three hours before the news came, the city collection department said 2,560 tons of paper had been frittered onto the streets. Twenty-five persons were in hospitals because of celebration accidents.

But all that was only the burning of the fuse to the explosive.

Peace! Shoot Only In A Friendly Way

San Francisco, Aug. 14 (AP)—"It looks like the war is over," Admiral Halsey said. "Cease firing, but if you see any enemy planes in the air, shoot them down in friendly fashion."

The hundreds of navy pilots, but a few seconds from their targets in the Tokyo area, heard and obeyed.

On Other Pages

Honolulu Celebrating Ever Since Friday

Honolulu, Aug. 14 (AP)—The same air-raid sirens which signaled the Japanese attack on Pearl Harbor, starting the war, sounded the end

(Continued on Page 4, Column 5)

HIROHITO TELLS FOE OF DEFEAT

Says 'Most Cruel Bomb' Could Destroy Civilization

New York, Wednesday Aug. 15 (AP)—The Japanese Cabinet issued today a "proclamation to the nation" calling on the Japanese people to obey Emperor Hirohito's imperial rescript announcing Japan's surrender to the Allied powers and pledging itself to do likewise, the Japanese Domei agency reported.

San Francisco, Aug. 14 (AP)—A Domei dispatch broadcast by the Tokyo Radio said tonight that Emperor Hirohito had told the Japanese people by radio that "the enemy had begun to employ a new and most cruel bomb" and should Japan continue to fight "it would lead to the total extinction of human civilization."

"The enemy has begun to employ a new and most cruel bomb, the power of which to do damage is indeed incalculable, taking the toll of many innocent lives," the Emperor was quoted as saying.

"Should we continue to fight, it would not only result in an ultimate collapse and the obliteration of the Japanese nation, but also it would lead to the total extinction of human civilization.

"Such being the case, how are we to save the millions of our subjects; or to alone ourselves before the hallowed spirits of our imperial ancestors? This is the reason we have ordered the acceptance of the joint declaration of the powers."

The Text Of The Rescript

The text of the rescript follows:

"To our good and loyal subjects:

"Pondering deeply the general trends of the world and the actual conditions of . . . (indistinct word) in our empire today, we have decided to effect a settlement of the present situation by resorting to an extraordinary measure.

We have ordered our Govern-

(Continued on Page 2, Column 4)

BULLETINS

London, Aug. 14 (AP)—King George VI will make a victory broadcast tomorrow (Wednesday) night at 9 P.M. (4 P.M. E.W.T.), following a thanksgiving service on the BBC at 8.15 P.M. (3.15 P.M. E.W.T.).

Manila, Wednesday, Aug. 15 (AP)—"I thank a merciful God that this mighty struggle is about to end," Gen. Douglas MacArthur commented this morning after receiving official notification of the Japanese capitulation and of his appointment as supreme Allied commander of occupation forces.

"I shall at once take steps to stop hostilities and further bloodshed.

New York, Wednesday, Aug. 15 (AP)—Japanese War Minister Korechika Anami has committed suicide, the Japanese Domei agency reported today. The English-language wireless broadcast was recorded by the Federal Communications Commission.

JAPS ACCEPT ALL TERMS, FIRING TO END AT ONCE, PRESIDENT ANNOUNCES

General MacArthur Is Named To Receive Surrender Of Enemy, Who Is Ordered To Comply With Any Requests He May Make

Guam, Wednesday, July 15 (AP)—Japanese aircraft are approaching the Pacific Fleet off Tokyo and are being shot down, Admiral Nimitz announced today. Five enemy planes have been destroyed since noon.

New York, Wednesday, Aug. 15 — Gen. Douglas MacArthur, in his first communication to Japan, has just ordered the Japanese Government and imperial general staff to put a radio station at his continuous disposal for communication of his orders to Japan, NBC's Merrill Mueller, radioed from MacArthur's headquarters in Manila today.

By DEWEY L. FLEMING

Washington, Aug. 14—The war with Japan ended tonight.

Japanese acceptance of Allied surrender terms, and orders for suspension of hostilities, were announced by President Truman at 7 P.M.

The news was announced in other Allied capitals at the same hour.

Gen. Douglas MacArthur, commander of United States Army forces in the Pacific, has been named supreme Allied commander to receive the formal Japanese surrender—at the earliest possible moment.

To Sign Surrender On Battleship

It is expected that the signing of the surrender instrument will take place aboard an American battleship.

The official proclamation of V-J day will await the formal signing of the surrender terms by Japan.

Although this proclamation may not come for several days, the President immediately granted a two-day holiday—tomorrow and Thursday—to all Federal employes in Washington and throughout the country.

This normally sedate capital went wild at the authentic news of the Japanese surrender. The downtown section was packed in anticipation of the announcement and the ensuing uproar was indescribable.

Truman Is Calm As He Calls Reporters

Perhaps the calmest person in the city, or so it seemed, was President Truman as he called reporters into his office at 7 P.M. and announced the news for which the world had been waiting.

Seated at his desk and showing no more excitement than if he were about to announce the appointment of a new postmaster at a Missouri village, he read a brief introductory statement before handing out the text of the Japanese reply to the Allied surrender ultimatum.

"I have received this afternoon a message from the Japanese Government," he began, "in reply to the message forwarded to that Government by the Secretary of State on August 11.

"I deem this reply a full acceptance of the Potsdam declaration which specifies the unconditional surrender of Japan. In the reply there is no qualification.

Arrangements Under Way For Signing

"Arrangements are now being made for the formal signing of surrender terms at the earliest possible moment.

"Gen. Douglas MacArthur has been appointed the supreme Allied commander to receive the Japanese surrender. Great Britain, Russia and China will be represented by high-ranking officers.

"Meantime, the Allied armed forces have been ordered to suspend offensive action.

"The proclamation of V-J day must wait upon the formal signing of the surrender terms by Japan."

Hull Arrives Late, Congratulates Truman

At that point the President began reading the text of the Japanese reply, as transmitted through the neutral Swiss Government. He said reporters need not try to take down the words in their notes as copies had been prepared for immediate distribution.

The text of the Japanese reply follows: "With reference to the Japanese Government's note of August 10 regarding their acceptance of the provisions of the Potsdam declaration and the reply of the governments of the United States, Great Britain, the Soviet Union and China sent by American Secretary of State Byrnes under the date of August 11, the Japanese Government have the honor to communicate to the governments of the four powers as follows:

"1. His Majesty the Emperor has issued an imperial rescript regarding Japan's acceptance of the provisions of the Potsdam declaration.

"2. His Majesty the Emperor is prepared to authorize and insure the signature by his Government and the imperial general headquarters of necessary terms for carrying out the provisions of the Potsdam declaration. His Majesty is also prepared to issue his commands to all the military, naval and air authorities of Japan and all the forces under their control wherever located to cease active

(Continued on Page 2, Column 1)

When the news was definite and final and at long last could be believed, more than a quarter of a million people flooded into the downtown streets leading into Sun Square, jamming traffic along Howard, Centre, Lexington, and Park. At about 10:00 p.m. war plants made it known that they would be closed, and the governor proclaimed the next day, Wednesday, the fifteenth, a legal holiday. East Baltimore Street's Block, usually brightly lit, suddenly fell dark and abandoned. "Closed" signs appeared on the doors of the strip joints. There was a bigger show going on.

Marie Lewandoski on the night of August 15, carrying Old Glory and the flag of the Free Polish.

Top, Uncle Sam (Attillio Allori) makes a mounted appearance in the celebration that animated Little Italy on August 15.

Right, A conga line forms on Charles Street, another example of the frivolity, delirium, and pent-up joy that erupted on V-J Day and night.

Along Pennsylvania Avenue, then the heart of Baltimore's African American community, celebrants keep the party going. Even so, for Frances Lockwood—wife of the black officer whose trip to Virginia to see him commissioned had meant that she had to move to the back of the bus—the memories were mixed. "When the war ended we all went out into the streets and shouted and embraced. It was a glad moment. There was a lot about the war I remember fondly—I met my soldier husband in it. But as a Negro, there was a lot that happened that I want to forget."

City celebrations were not confined to downtown and Sun Square—many neighborhoods took it on their own to organize what came to be known as block parties. As the servicemen came home, back to their old neighborhoods, residents would shut off the street at either end of a given block, hang pennants (as pictured, on Randall Street), set up tables, and do potluck. Families brought their returning sons and daughters (some still in uniform, some in civilian clothes but sporting the famous "ruptured duck" discharge pin on their clothes) to the party, where the veterans gorged themselves on the food they said they had missed—hot dogs, hamburgers, Mom's apple pie. In some cases, small bands played the songs that helped define their years away: "Don't sit under the apple tree with anyone else but me, 'til I come marching home." Marching home they came—to the very neighborhood block they'd left!

George Wills remembers V-J Day well, as a final farewell to the war. That August he and most of the McDonogh boys were up in the woods at Camp Red Cloud, the school summer retreat on Lake Champlain. "Doc Lamborn announced to campers that 'peace is here.' He added solemnly that 'we all have to remember not to let this kind of war ever happen again.'"

But about the day he came home—I will never forget it

About Sgt. Bernard B. Blum, shot down over Yugoslavia in May 1944. His wife, Shirley Kirsh Blum, had been notified in September of 1944 that her husband was alive but a prisoner of war in Germany; she heard nothing further. In January of 1945 Mrs. Blum received a visitor, Lt. Walter Sabastian of Chicago. He asked to see Mrs. Blum because he had been a member of the flight crew when her husband's plane had gone down. He said that Sergeant Blum had been wounded by flak, explaining that shrapnel had hit his leg, and first aid, such as it was, was administered in the plane. While the crew was bailing out, Sergeant Blum lost consciousness, and the crew decided to *throw* him out, while one of the crew pulled the ripcord.

On May 3, 1945, Mrs. Blum received a cablegram from her husband saying that he was alive and well at Camp Lucky Strike, near Le Havre, France. A few weeks later she received a letter from him saying he would be home soon.

And he was—in mid-August 1945, and I know this because, after making at least thirty phone calls in the hopes of finding Mrs. Blum, I found her. Mrs. Blum is, at this writing, alive and well and was happy to talk with me about her late husband's ordeal and homecoming. She added a few details to the story, and corrected a few others.

"When he parachuted out of the plane he didn't land in Yugoslavia, as the *Sun* reported. It was in Albania. He also told me that a farmer saw him hit the ground and came running out to meet him. The farmer, my husband recalled, appeared to be friendly and hospitable and even took him into his farmhouse, served him a meal, and tried to make him comfortable. He said that there was a doctor living nearby and he would go and bring him to provide the medical help Bernard badly needed. But, it turned out, the farmer didn't go for a doctor; instead, he went for the police—who immediately arrested Bernard and took him into custody. Within weeks he was a prisoner in Stalag 17—the German prison camp made famous in the movie of the same name.

"But about the day he came home. I will never forget it. It was during a hot spell in August 1945. We had a shore home down on the Magothy River, and so our family went down there to spend few days. One day, in the middle of the afternoon, we heard a car coming up the road, and shouting coming from it. We went out to take a look to see what the commotion was all about. We saw a few heads poking out of the car windows, the passengers hollering and waving their arms.

One of those hollering and waving was, it would turn out, my husband! He had gone to our house in the city, didn't find me, and with others in my family, headed for the shore home.

"Well, we fell in each other's arms—like dead weights. We stayed clinging, tightly, for I don't know how long. Of course we both cried. As I remember, the family had to pry us apart."

It will never be the same again without them

Just before the war ended in 1945, an announcement sealed the fate of the Charles Street double-deckers: Edmund Collins, vice president of Fifth Avenue Coach Company, which provided Baltimore with its double-decker fleet, announced that "the day of the double-decker in Baltimore is finished." The company planned to stop production.

In a stinging editorial in the *Evening Sun*, R. P. Harriss spoke for an enraged citizenry. "When we took that last ride back in 1942 we were told that removing the double-deckers was a wartime measure only. Recently it was announced that New York's Fifth Avenue double-decker will be replaced after the war with single-decker affairs, and so I called the local transit company here and was given absolutely no assurance that the Charles Street double-decker would come back. I say, give us back our double-deckers."

"Ah, those elegant days back in the twenties when open tops were in operation!" he lamented on July 25, 1945. "On a fine spring afternoon, with the feathery green showing on the trees on North Charles, a fellow could sit up there with a Goucher gal and think beautiful thoughts." Sitting up on the top deck, a low-hanging branch would force his date and him to duck, making for a "mild adventure"; he closed with undisguised remorse: "These double-deckers certainly gave Charles Street a grand air it has lacked ever since they were taken off. It will never be the same again without them."

It never was.

I wondered if even in the end of his life he was still waking up screaming in the night

In 1941, sixteen-year-old William Goldstein was living at 3505 North Charles Street and was in his room on the second floor that Sunday morning, December 7, 1941, when, at about 12:30, he heard his father and mother call frantically to him, "Come down here! Come down here!" They explained in hurried terms that the Japanese had bombed Pearl Harbor and that the country was now at war.

He was a student at Baltimore City College, and the war was far away until a few months later, when his brother joined the marines. Within a few years the war would come home to Bill Goldstein with a personal experience so vivid he would remember the war for the rest of his life.

He was graduated from City in 1942 and matriculated at Washington College in Chestertown, on the Eastern Shore. He recalled this chapter of his life:

"You knew the country was at war because the campus life reflected it. All of us were in ROTC, and there was always talk of speeding up our studies, and when and where, and in what form, our life in the military would be. Students were dropping out of school and going into service. You never knew when you went to class who had enlisted.

"But the most compelling way you got to understand that the country was at war was the sight, on this small college campus on the Eastern Shore of Maryland, of guys who had come back from the war zones—missing an arm or a leg, or both. There were students in wheelchairs and students on crutches and students with canes—they were the guys who had been in the war and had been wounded, and discharged, and came back to school, some in their early twenties, as beginning freshmen.

"The reality of the war came home to me in a very powerful way when I discovered that I was assigned a roommate who had lost a leg, and that he would be sleeping in the bottom bunk, I was to take the top. We got along fine. I learned to help him dress and undress and get around, without offending him. But some of the nights were bad.

"His name was Wayne Causey, and he was a paratrooper with the Eighty-second Airborne. He told me that he had been a part of Operation Market Garden, an attempt by the Western Allies on September 17, 1944, to land three airborne divisions behind German lines at Nijmegen and Eindhoven, in the Netherlands, with the aim of seizing a bridge at Arnheim.

"After an eight-day battle they had taken the bridge, although the Germans eventually got it back. More than six thousand of the original thirty-five thousand men were taken prisoner; two thousand succeeded in crossing the Rhine to safety; fourteen hundred airborne troops had been killed. The casualties were high. Wayne Causey was one of them.

The morning after Wednesday, August 15, the street cleaners were left to clean up the confetti and the noise-makers and the memories they held of four long years of war. It was, at long last, over. Over there, over here.

"Often during the night he would wake up screaming, yelling, and thrashing round in the bunk below, 'Watch out! Watch out!' and 'Let's get the hell out of here!' and 'Look out! Look out!'

"Wayne graduated and went to the University of Maryland School of Law and practiced over on the Eastern Shore. I wondered, as he grew older, if he was still waking up screaming in the middle of the night, reliving his paratroop jump and his days in battle behind enemy lines in that dreadful September of 1944.

"I heard that he had died. And I wondered if even in the end of his life he was still waking up screaming in the night."

Afterword

About my own homecoming: In August of 1945, I was still serving aboard the USS *Leonis,* then a part of the massive fleet gathering in Leyte Gulf in the Philippines, readying for the invasion of Japan—we were to invade Kyushu in September. But after August 6 and 9, following the United States' dropping of atomic bombs on Hiroshima and Nagasaki, the war at long last came to an end. We were ordered (September 4) to Ulithi, in the Caroline Islands, and (September 8) to San Pedro (Los Angeles) to pick up soldiers and marines. From there, we were ordered (October 15) to Panama, through the Canal (October 29) to Norfolk, Virginia—then (December 3), by the most incredible of coincidences, to Baltimore, at Port Covington. We held decommissioning services the morning of December 5, and with that same commission pennant as a souvenir (I still have it) I found my way to a streetcar and went home (I knew the way, all right)—to where I was living with my parents, at 3608 Cottage Avenue, in northwest Baltimore. As it turned out, I'd left Baltimore on December 7, 1942, and I came home to Baltimore on December 5, 1945. Three years, almost to the day.

Former USO hostesses Sonia Fox Schnaper and Charlotte Shenk are, at this writing, alive and well. Mrs. Schnaper served at the USO at 305 West Monument; Mrs. Shenk, at the USO at Saratoga and Cathedral. They shared with me their vivid memories of serving pot-luck dinners and dancing to "Kiss me once and kiss me twice and kiss me once again, it's been a long, long time..."

Sgt. Jim Bready, who preached the joy of hitchhiking from nearby army bases to Baltimore and back, is, at this writing, alive and well.

Late in the war, before shipping out for the European Theater, Sergeant Bready married "the pert, red-haired young lady behind the desk" in the Govans library, Mary Hortop, at Govans Presbyterian Church. Sixty-seven years and three sons later, they remain lovingly married.

Reuben Shiling, who fought the battle of the Office of Price Administration in Baltimore's "Little Washington," was interviewed for this book only days before he died in 2008, a kind man with an agile mind that was a storehouse of memories of Baltimore in World War II.

Jean Rubin Levitas, who was eighteen years old in 1942 and lived in Pimlico but worked the shifts at Eastern Aviation on Broening Highway, surfaced in 2009. The occasion was the Rosie the Riveters Association National Convention, Friday, June 20, at the Burkshire Marriott Conference Hotel in Baltimore, and she was pictured in the *Sun* along with three other Rosies. The *Sun* reported that the association would be hosting a "Rosie the Riveter Musical" and a USO-style dance, featuring music of the 1940s. Seventy "Rosies" (including Mrs. Levitas) who worked the shifts in wartime Baltimore and who were still living in the area made it to the reunion that night.

I was not at that reunion but was invited to another one—nine girls who graduated from Forest Park High School in 1941, the June before war broke out, and who lived through a lot of this. They told stories about how the war had changed their lives—how some had filled in the lonely times at the USO and how some wartime romances had been formed there. One said, "I married my husband in 1943; he was in the army. He left for overseas shortly afterward. When he came home in 1946 he was not the same guy. He had been taken prisoner. He limped from shrapnel in his leg. He was depressed. He died when he was only forty-seven." Another said, "Married life during the war was different. Many of us moved to the base where our husbands were stationed. I moved to an apartment near the base in Monroe, Louisiana." Another, "My boyfriend enlisted in the Army Air Corps and he was sent to Wichita Falls, Texas. Like so many of the girls in those days, I followed my husband to wherever he was stationed in the States, until about a year later, when he was sent overseas to the Burma Theater. I went home and moved back in with my mother. There was nothing else I could do." Another, "My husband was sent on a secret mission. When he came home, he committed suicide."

Happily, at this writing, William Goldstein, Robert Rappaport,

Katherine Fletcher, John Kopper, Ed Snyder, Maurice Paper, Norvell Miller, Frances Lockwood, George Wills, and Mildred Keiser Strutt are alive to share their memories.

I lost track of certain of my interviewees and have not been able to track them down following our several conversations. Included among the missing are James Gentry, Ronald Flitt, and Sarah Dittinger Chandler.

Sadly, Hy Pusin, Reuben Shiling, Mrs. Louisa Reynolds, and Mrs. Charles Peace have passed on.

Acknowledgments

This book is as much the work of Paul McCardell, librarian of the *Baltimore Sun,* and Jeff Korman, director of the Maryland Department of the Enoch Pratt Free Library, as it is mine. Each is a Baltimore historian and an accomplished researcher in his own right. I am in awe of their collective command of the subject, and I am deeply appreciative of their commitment to getting this book out. I acknowledge the sure and guiding hand of Dr. Robert J. Brugger, senior editor at the Johns Hopkins University Press, whose idea the book was in the first place and whose suggestions have led me through home front Baltimore day by day and page by page.

I am grateful for the careful, critical, and unsparing readings of the manuscript in its several stages by Dr. Emile Bendit, Sarajane Greenfeld, Norvell Miller, Dr. Elisa New (professor of American literature at Harvard), longtime *Sun* writers Jim Bready and Fred Rasmussen, Neil A. Grauer (former *Baltimore News-American* reporter and author), Dr. Sol Snyder, Wayne Schaumburg, Efrem Potts, and (yes!) eleven-year-old World War II buff Leah Smith. Their sharp pencils and agile minds have enriched the story and caught some howlers. I am indebted to the helpful researchers at the Maryland Rail Heritage Library: Dennis Falter, Jerry Kelly, Henry "Pete" Riecks, Rev. Edward Schell, Kenneth Spencer, Norman Janssen, and Charles Plantholt; and, at the Maryland Historical Society, all of the genial, hard-working, and accommodating staff. I thank, too, Leslie Sandler, who has been an able and patient researcher and typist, and Carol Greif Sandler, for allowing me to use the poem by her grandmother, Amy Greif, about the Trans Lux.

Finally, I owe thanks to the many people who, though they have no standing as editors or researchers, lived in Baltimore during those sometimes frenetic and always uncertain times and saw it all happen (as I did not). Their memories helped me understand the era from so many differing perspectives.

Sources

Newspapers, we have come to believe, are the first draft of history; this book, then, which has largely been drawn from the pages of the *Baltimore Sun* (morning, evening, Sunday), the *Baltimore News-Post,* and the *Baltimore Afro-American,* can be said to be a second draft of the history of home front Baltimore in World War II.

In particular, the World War II Service Edition of the *Sun* proved especially useful. The *Afro-American* has been a particularly rich resource, covering events in the African American community in a way that the *Sun* and *News-Post* did not.

As for my sources for what was happening over there (in contrast with what was happening over here), I have relied heavily on Chris Bishop and Chris McNab, *Campaigns of World War II, Day by Day* (London: Amber Books, 2007); Martin Gilbert, *The Second World War* (New York: Henry Holt, 1989); Richard Lingeman, *"Don't You Know There's a War On?": The American Home Front, 1941-1945* (New York: Thunder's Mouth Press/Nation's Books, 1970); Elizabeth Michener, *War Stories: Remembering World War II* (New York: Berkeley Publishing/Penguin Group, 2002); Donald L. Miller, *D-Days in the Pacific* (New York: Simon & Schuster, 1945); C. L. Sulzberger, revised and updated by Stephen Ambrose, *A New History of World War II* (New York: American Heritage, 1997); Studs Terkel, *The Good War* (New York: New Press, 1984); David White and Daniel Murphy, *The Everything World War II Book: People, Places, Battles, and All the Key Events,* 2nd ed. (Avon, MA: Adams Media, 2007).

Index

Page numbers in italics refer to photographs.